Published by TWH Publishing
www.thewritinghall.co.uk

Cover design: Stephen Caile

ISBN 978-1-9998669-5-2

Eat. Sleep. Control. Repeat.

By Sophie Mei Lan

Using self-love, not self-harm, to be truly successful

To all those who struggle to fit in yet strive to succeed in holistic health and happiness. You may feel a 'misfit', but it's because you stand out from the crowd. You're a change-maker, which is why people try to dull your sparkle.

It's because they can see you shining. They know that your past makes you remarkable. They know that the damage you've suffered makes you even more beautiful.

Never dim your light for anyone. Let go of the vampires in your life and make way for the cheerleaders.

This book is dedicated to my support network, who have all somehow helped me to survive and thrive.

To my parents, siblings and family — who instilled the fire inside me. The healthcare and fitness professionals who keep me physically and mentally strong. To my online community of rebellious souls, and my self-help groups.

To you, reader…I've experienced the very best — and worst — that life has to offer. You're hearing me, listening to me, and giving authentic voices like mine power and purpose.

To my sisterhood of cheerleading women, whose journeys continue to inspire me to keep dancing along my own wonderfully weird path. To the main women in my life, now and for eternity…my daughters.

Live a life of love, smiles and sparkle — from the inside out.

Peace, Love and Shimmies

Sophie Mei Lan, a.k.a Mama Mei

Foreword by Eamonn Holmes

Eat. Sleep. Control. Repeat. is an amazingly insightful, gripping read. It just goes to show that we never know what is happening behind someone else's closed doors.

I feel very guilty that I only knew Sophie Mei Lan as a beautiful young woman who had a wonderful personality and for whom the world seemed her oyster, but none of us know the true lives of others.

Society focuses on appearances too much, for both men and women, and mental health is talked about but often forgotten when it comes to how we treat one another.

Whilst this is a sad, gritty and brave tale of addiction and eating disorders, it also offers hope that, no matter how bad things get or how bad mental illness and addictive behaviours become, there is always a way out.

Often, we all have to 'put on a brave face', but Sophie's honesty is truly inspiring, and I hope men and women alike read the book and are encouraged by her recovery journey and know that, with the right help and support, there's always a future.

Prologue: The bully inside me

I achieved what I thought was success. I realised all my study, business and professional goals — surpassed them, in fact.

But I was so focused on a blossoming career in the media and entertainment industry that I paid the ultimate sacrifice.

Me.

Often the worst bully is within us. The person who bullies us most is ourselves. Without realising, we can become our own worst enemy, our own abusive boss, and be plagued with self-hatred and loathing.

I have written this book because my 'best friend' — i.e. my own thoughts — nearly killed me. Today, I feel lucky to be alive, and I want to share with you how I won the fight.

*

My best friend was my eating disorder, my crutch. My best friend helped me reach career highs I could only dream of. But my best friend was also my biggest bully.

I loved my best friend and I didn't think I could live without her. But the more I spent time with her, the more I started to believe her. The more I bullied myself until I was 'the worst bulimic' medics had ever seen.

My best friend and I became one. She controlled my life. She was the bully inside me.

Like a lot of ambitious people, I used negative coping strategies. Things that gave me comfort but a false sense of security. To the outside world I achieved so much — a job in TV and radio, a professional dance career that allowed me to travel the world, and my own multi-award-winning businesses. I had it all. Or so it seemed.

If you're like me, a highly driven, passionate and so-called successful person, you will also know that, deep down, until we achieve happiness within ourselves, our career goals feel empty.

Deep down, we just long to be loved. We long to feel content and we long to feel whole.

You can get there. You can get to a stage in your life where you're ambitious but also content. Successful at work and, most importantly, in life. Holistically successful.

How do I know this?

After a long rollercoaster of a journey, I'm finally on the summit of holistic success.

I've not had a picture-perfect life, as you'll discover should you continue to read. I've experienced some of the worst abuse possible. I've battled many demons and I've attempted suicide on several occasions.

I'm fortunate to still be here to tell my story. I feel this is my calling…to show you how I went from a life of self-harm and destruction to my life today, as a thriving business owner, a health and wellbeing 'influencer', a mum of two and friend to many.

Much of my story revolves around my eating disorder and my battle with anorexia and bulimia. This, I now realise, was my way of controlling a world in which I felt out of control. My eating disorder was my dirty secret but also my best friend.

You may not have an eating disorder, but some other physical manifestation of controlling thoughts and your own internal bully. You will no doubt still relate to my thought processes and feelings.

These days, I've learnt to live without my best friend. I sometimes mourn her, but I feel so much better now I'm in control of my life.

I no longer lead a double life. I no longer need to pretend I can cope. I no longer try to fit in. I have embraced who I am, and I am no longer embarrassed of my past, my present or how I want to see my future.

I hope that, by hearing the candid darkness of my story and the light I've now achieved, you will be inspired to become holistically successful, too.

You can achieve inner peace whilst still on your journey. Enjoy the ride, rather than just focusing on the destination at all costs.

You can manage the pain you feel so intensely inside. You don't have to work so hard. You don't have to hate yourself so much. You can achieve your career goals whilst still being healthy.

I never thought I would begin to heal. I never thought that this pain inside would ever subside. I never thought I'd cope without my eating disorder. I never thought I'd enjoy the journey. I never thought I'd escape the insidious cycle of my 'successful' career.

But I did, and I'm thriving more than ever. I'm free to be me, not who the world wants me to be. Together, we can do this.

'You haven't come this far to only come this far.'

CHAPTER ONE

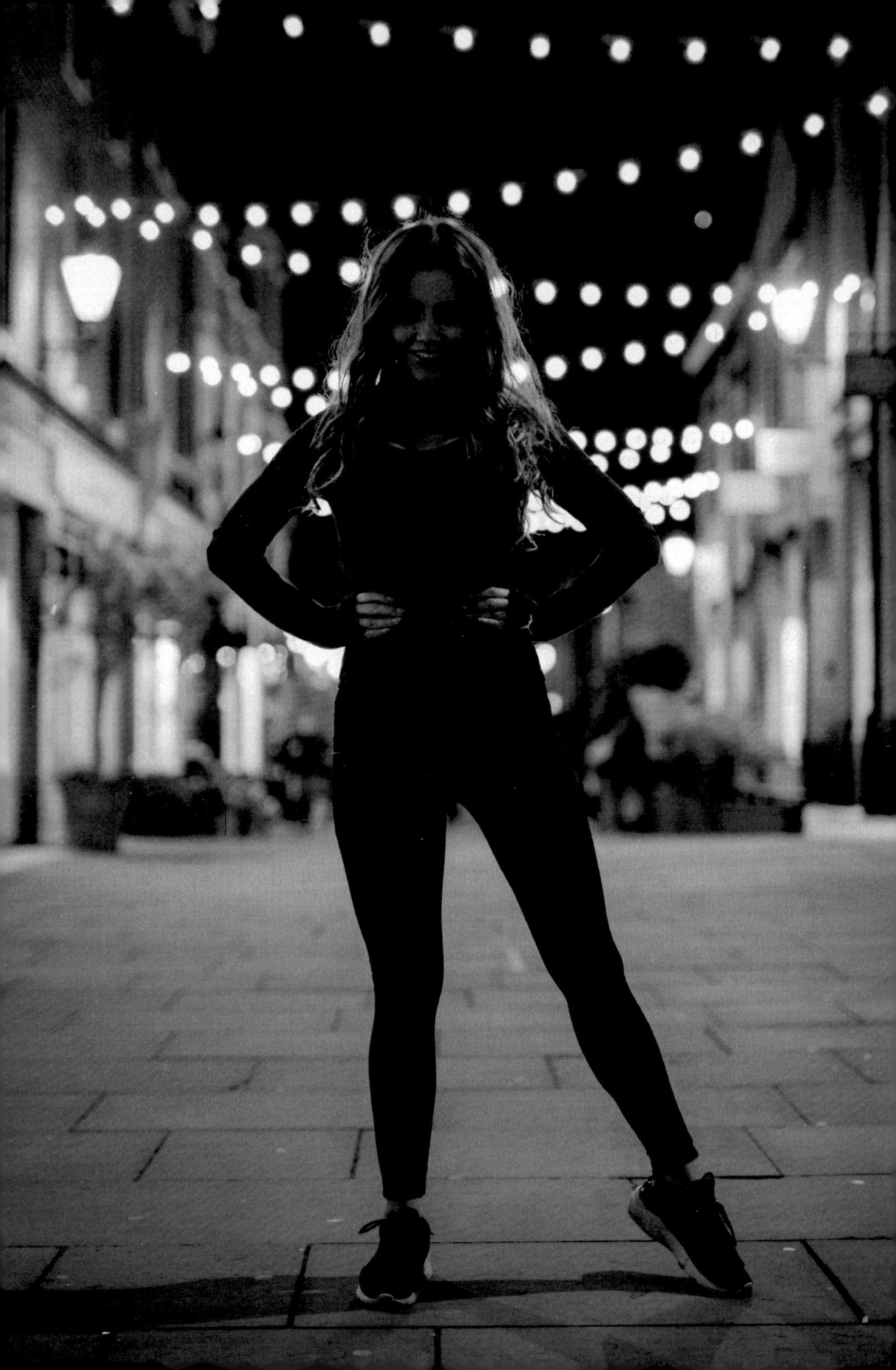

'The most beautiful people we have known are those who have known defeat, known suffering, known struggle, known loss, and have found their way out of the depths. These persons have an appreciation, a sensitivity, and an understanding of life that fills them with compassion, gentleness, and a deep loving concern. Beautiful people do not just happen.' ~ Elisabeth Kübler-Ross

Bent over double and clawing my nails deep into my throat, I was determined to get every bit of food and fluid out of my body.

I wasn't in a nice shiny bathroom making myself sick quietly, like people do on TV. I was in an attic, and I regularly threw up into a mop bucket.

My computer glared at me through the darkness. On paper I was 'successful'. I had a promising career in the media, I was a well-known professional dancer, yet there I was, clutching a bucket filled with bile, a bin full of wrappers and crumbs in the corner.

What had my life become?

I'd begun to achieve most things I'd aspired to, in terms of my career. It didn't stop me feeling alone. Feeling a total mess.

I wasn't physically alone. I'd recently moved back in with my mum and stepdad because I couldn't manage living on my own.

Despite my bulimic habits, I still endured casual relationships. I had friends and I was inundated with career opportunities. But my face said it all. My cheeks became swollen from constant purging. My bowels were dysfunctional, due to regular laxative overdoses. I spent all my wages on slimming pills, fake hair, false nails and masses of healthy food and fizzy drinks.

I'd strived for this life, this career, but this was not the success I'd dreamed of.

Back then, I worked as a PR and social media marketing account manager. I promoted large organisations like the NHS. In my breaks, I'd write articles for newspapers, then, after work, I taught people to belly-dance or I'd perform in a dance show. I even presented my own TV documentary.

Maybe this was what people meant by 'having it all'?

The only thing that kept me going was a promise to myself that I would soon die. That was my only comfort, that I could take my own life when things got too much.

And it did become too much. I couldn't cope with the double life. I couldn't cope with toxic relationships and men using me, as well as the abuse I gave myself. I couldn't cope with trying to be a successful career woman whilst killing myself behind closed doors.

*

My eating disorder began when I was eleven, though I didn't get a diagnosis until I was in my teens. When I first went to my G.P., aged fourteen, I was told that I looked 'fit and healthy'. Apparently, there wasn't anything for anyone to be concerned about. (Today, a number of medical experts agree that most people with an eating disorder have a normal BMI or they're overweight.)

My treatment began when I was eighteen, though I'd battled with bulimia for a number of years by then. It was the crutch I'd relied on to get me through my school years and exams — through bullying and through abuse. It was my main coping mechanism and it had an insidious grip on me. It became my whole world.

On paper and in the media I may have been seen as successful. I'd been a semi-finalist on 'Britain's Got Talent', I'd presented a TV documentary in Egypt, and I was studying philosophy and Italian at the University of Manchester. Until that point, I'd had a 'normal' BMI. When I went to live in Italy as part of my degree, however, my weight plummeted.

At nineteen, my dream year abroad came to an abrupt end. A skeletal mess, I was forced to return home. My body finally demonstrated what was going on internally. Whilst people assumed that this was when my eating disorder was at its worse, due to the way I looked, they couldn't have been more wrong.

Back in the U.K., it was easier to access treatment when I weighed less, though the scales didn't fully reflect how gaunt I was. My BMI was a curse — the biggest barrier towards getting the help I so desperately needed.

Despite finally receiving help, I admit that I ignored a lot of it. I was too far gone when it came to listening to, and trusting, my eating disorder — the only 'person' I believed knew me inside out.

My diet and eating patterns were chaotic and I was obsessed with exercise, due to my addictive personality. Finally, after years of self-harm, my eating disorder had full control.

I was an incontinent youth addicted to laxatives who'd overdose on diet pills and 'healthy food'.

My disease almost killed me.

It didn't matter to me — as long as I could throw up and rid myself of every morsel of food that had entered my body, I was okay.

*

Looking back now, I often wonder where my destructive thoughts began, where they came from.

Was my eating disorder the result of nature or nurture?

CHAPTER TWO

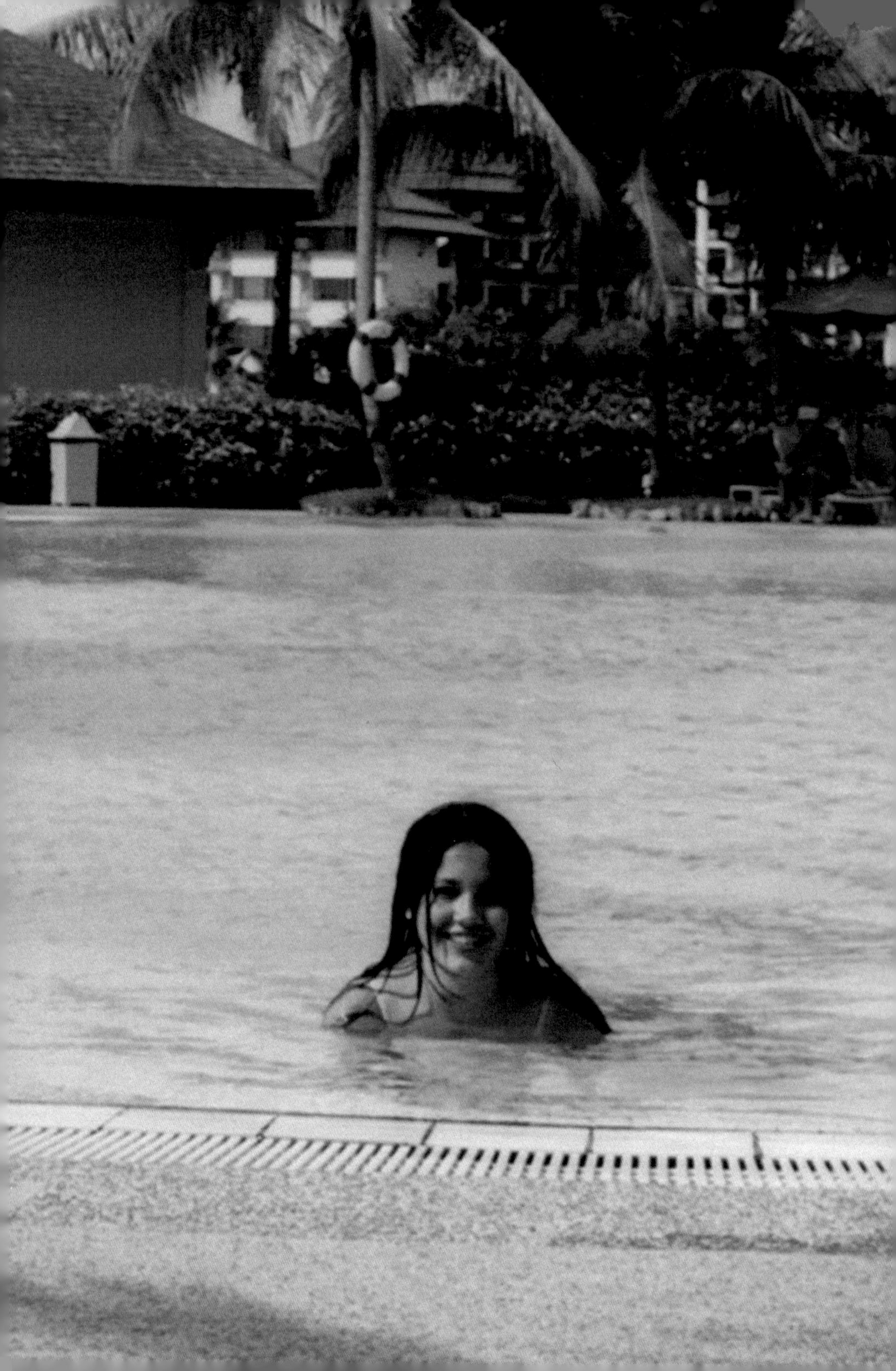

'The emerging woman...will be strong-minded, strong-hearted, strong-souled, and strong-bodied...strength and beauty must go together.'
~ Louisa May Alcott

As a child I desperately wanted to fit in. I didn't belong to any one group of people, for a number of reasons. I think my feelings of being an outsider stemmed from the fact that I'm mixed race (the fancy term is 'dual heritage').

I grew up in a diverse, multicultural neighbourhood in Sheffield. Instead of celebrating its differences, however, it always felt multi-segmented. Sadly, there wasn't a segment for people like me.

I'm both English and Chinese. I always tick the 'other' box on forms, despite never setting foot in China.

Mum took me and my sister to 'Chinese School' at weekends, the idea being that we could connect with people who also had an oriental heritage. I still felt the odd one out there. I wasn't bilingual either, like most of the others, who spoke Mandarin or Cantonese.

My Chinese family live in Malaysia — a British colony — so they're fluent in English. Though I'm only half-Chinese, I feel disconnected from other ethnic minorities, but also from 'full' English people.

I didn't know which part of me to disown. I craved to be one or the other — English or Chinese. Being dual heritage just made me feel like I didn't belong anywhere.

My mum took us to Malaysia each year to visit our Chinese relatives. I loved these visits, but I felt tall and broad in comparison to my extended family. They envied my stature, my paler skin and my lighter hair.

In many ways I felt at home in Malaysia, more so than I did in the U.K. at that time. I loved how the humid heat suited my body, how the spicy food and flavours tickled my palate, and I felt a deep connection with the people and the place.

Yet Yorkshire was where I was born and raised. It also felt like home. Having an attachment to both races meant I didn't quite belong to either as a whole person.

Why couldn't I just fit in?

My heritage is hugely important to me. My race is constantly on display from my facial features. In childhood I learned to loathe the way I looked. I hated my face.

I longed to resemble models in magazines. I longed to be thin. I dreamt of having blonde hair, blue eyes and an oval face. I thought that all my problems would go away if I could just look like the people I followed in the media.

It wasn't just my origin that made me stand out from the crowd. The fact that my parents had separated and lived apart was another cause for attention back then.

I was a 'suitcase kid', passing from house to house, family to family, home to home. I had two of everything: two toothbrushes, two wardrobes, two lots of toys and two sets of parents.

I was actually lucky to have so much love and an abundance of material objects. But the confusion of living at two homes and negotiating a challenging school life was tough. My older sister was my only constant; we went to the same school and had the same family set up.

At that time, you didn't come across many families in which the parents had divorced. Whilst some people said we were blessed to have two lives, others classed us as being from a broken home.

I hated that term; in my mind, though I came from an unconventional family, I believe that it's better for children to be brought up in two relatively peaceful homes, rather than under one roof — if their parents are in an unloving, fractious relationship.

Despite what the outside world and media thought of our situation, in both homes there was love. None of these differences was an issue for me to accept, but when you're young and impressionable, you want to stand with the masses, not stand out.

Prejudice against our family really kicked in when people in our area discovered that my dad was gay. It hadn't been a secret — or even something that I'd really thought about. I simply accepted that my mum lived with a man and so did my dad.

My dad came out as gay when I was three. The beauty of young children includes their innocence and open minds. Kids may ask questions, but they largely accept what's put in front of them. It's society that feeds prejudice and intolerance.

Perhaps unsurprisingly, when I started junior school, I was selective with the details I shared, relating to my home life — I somehow knew that it wasn't the norm.

To the outside world, we described my dad's partner as his lodger. This is not at all how we viewed him behind closed doors; he was very much part of our family — we felt lucky to have an extra dad. I remember contributing to a book about children with gay parents and being asked what was unique about our family. 'My dad's partner jokes with us and calls us pigs. He's funny,' I said.

I had absolutely no issue with my dad being gay. Why would something that was so natural to me be a problem? My beliefs didn't cause any damage, only the views of others.

We lived in a poor suburb of Sheffield, and whilst my local community was culturally diverse, it was not as accepting of people if they weren't heterosexual.

A schoolfriend's parents found out the truth about my dad's 'lodger'. They were subsequently banned from visiting our house and other parents were warned, too.

Sadly, that was not our family's only experience of homophobia. The abuse was harder to manage; a couple of decades ago, nobody really took issue if a person was homophobic. It felt so unjust to me; how could something that didn't impact anyone else cause so much controversy?

The only way I could deal with the injustices of the world — over which I had no control — was to strictly govern anything to do with my body. That was something I did have authority over.

I detested the skin I was in. I thought that if I could change aspects of myself, I would feel better about everything.

That was the start of a very slippery slope. Though I wasn't aware of it then, I'd just taken my first steps towards self-destruction.

CHAPTER THREE

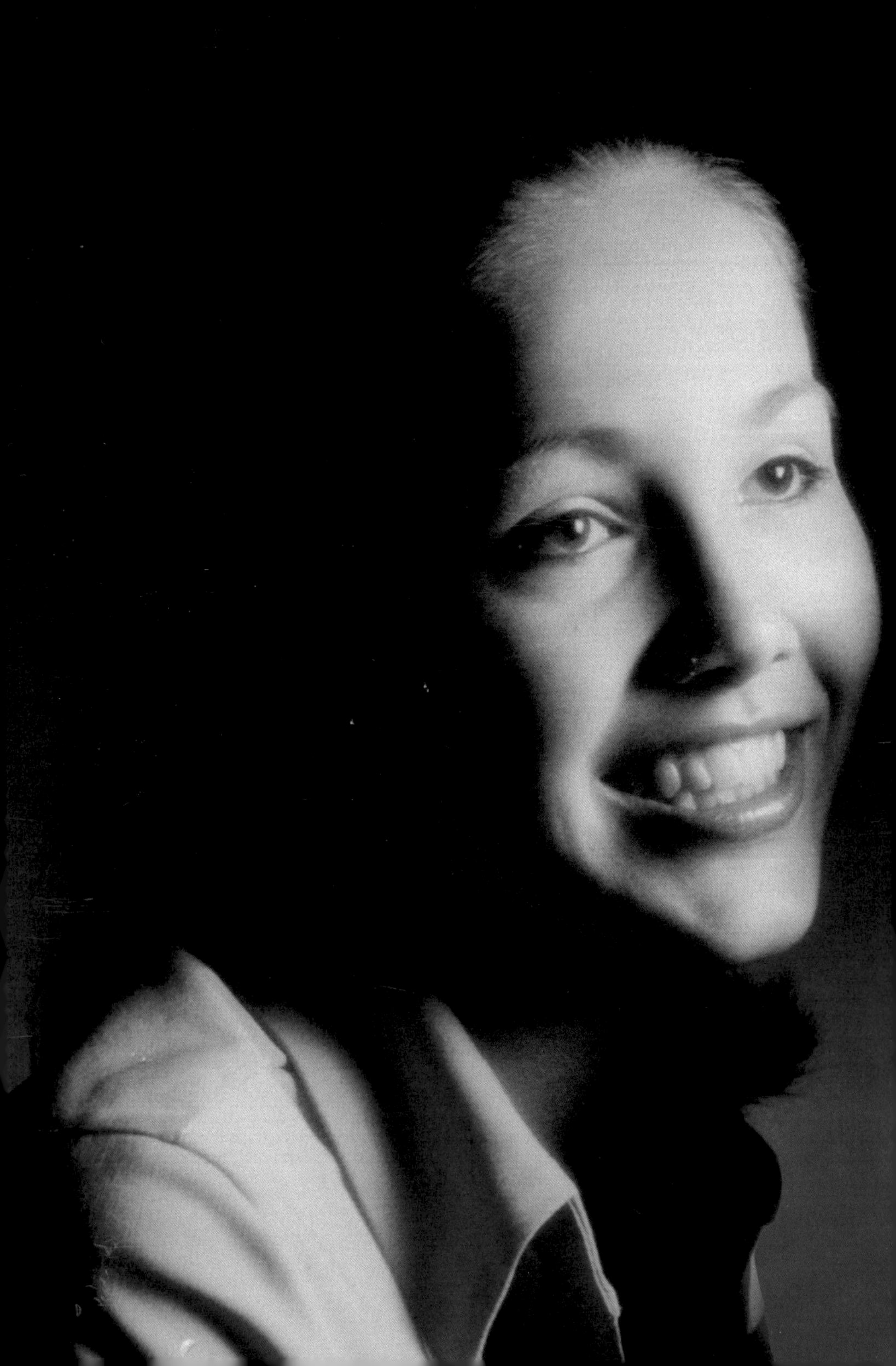

'I am beautiful, no matter what they say. Words can't bring me down. I am beautiful, in every single way. Yes, words can't bring me down. So, don't you bring me down today.'
~ 'Beautiful' by Christina Aguilera

I hated my face and my broad body disgusted me. My shame built to a crescendo, and that was when I first dug my fingers into my throat to make myself sick.

I was eleven, and I'd just started senior school. It wasn't long before the high school bullies spotted my weaknesses. They knew I was uncomfortable with how I looked.

Standing out at school can be empowering if it's an active decision, but quite frightening if it's unintended. And though you may look back and see it as a positive later in life, it doesn't feel so rosy when you're living through it—when suffering, within the confines of narrow corridors and grim, foul-smelling toilets.

I was called 'moon head' and 'flat face'. The bullies regularly pulled my hair or slashed my coat. They'd draw their eyelids back with their fingers and taunt me with their 'slanty eyes'. Consciously or unconsciously, they bullied me for being mixed race, for appearing differently to them and not fitting in.

I loathed my flat face, my chubby cheeks, my big smile and my small eyes. I had a big head (not in the metaphorical sense) and dark, poker-straight hair. I was big boned, curvy and tall.

I dreamt of being petite and small like my Chinese relatives, though I also wanted my face to be oval rather than round, and my hair to be blonde and my eyes blue—the Western ideal.

I endured bullying throughout my teens and almost came to accept it. What pushed me over the edge was when the bullies infiltrated my home, via text and voicemail.

I'd just got my first mobile phone—an electronic brick by today's standards. Whilst this gave me new-found freedom, it also enabled others to invade my privacy.

The thing with mobile phones and tablets is that anyone can intrude into your safe space. They provide greater opportunities

13

for bullies' cruel words to stab and slice. Before then, the bullying had been limited to school and my bus journeys home, but now I didn't feel safe or secure anywhere.

One day, I was lying on the sofa watching a kids' programme after school when my phone alerted me to a text. It said, 'You're a fat ugly bitch, you should be ashamed.'

How could they still get to me? I was surrounded by my loving family, yet I felt alone and vulnerable. My whole body froze. A fog cast over my brain and I felt physically sick.

My school life was already hell. I suffered daily racist and homophobic chants: 'moon face'; 'ugly chink'; 'your dad's a battyman'; 'you're a fat, ugly slut, you deserve to be abused'. And so on. But now these comments weren't just coming home with me in my mind — I was constantly reminded via text how much some people wanted to destroy me.

It became more than name-calling. It led to threats and physical violence on the bus to and from school. There was no escape.

So many times I wanted to die. Teachers only saw it as a disagreement between classmates, but how was it an argument when all I did was receive the abuse? It's like I 'asked for it' by simply existing.

Once inside a cubicle in the school toilets, I'd claw at my arms and legs with my nails, wishing I could destroy my body, my skin…my whole self. School didn't represent the best days of my life — I felt that death would be a better option.

Suffice to say, I wasn't part of the popular group at school. I had a real mix of friends and liked to be surrounded by nice and interesting people. Not belonging to one specific group meant I was prone to bullying…I had no one to protect me, as most of my friends were being bullied, too.

I found solace in drama and dancing. I still didn't fit into certain groups, but at least I got into most clubs due to my 'diverse background'. I helped organisations tick their boxes.

Every moment on stage was sacred. It gave me the opportunity to be someone else. I could escape the body and face that made me a target, a 'freak'.

One evening, in 2001, I was watching telly with my mum and stepdad. A reality show came on called 'Popstars'. On the programme I saw a girl who looked like me.

I couldn't believe it. She was prettier than I was, but she had similar features. From that moment, the reality TV star, opera singer and violinist Myleene Klass became my role model. Vanessa Mae was an inspiration, too.

I started to wear green eye make-up, just as Myleene did on the programme. I may have been biased, but I could see the beauty of her ethnicity as well as her talent.

As Myleene's popularity grew, so did mine. Boys began to fancy me, and I dated some of the 'in' crowd. Though I hadn't been popular before at school, I became so by association.

Some of the popular girls didn't like this, and so the bullying began again. They called me a geek, a 'goody two shoes'…said I didn't fit in with them. I didn't want to fit in; I had my own friends—fellow 'odd-bods'—who I cared about, and I wasn't going to drop them to be part of the popular gang. Those odd-bod friendships were important to me then and they still are now; two decades on, one of them remains a very close friend, ally, and an important part of my trusted inner circle.

*

Now in my thirties, I've forgiven the bullies and moved on— though they've never apologised for what they put me through in my teens, and I'll never forget their torturous ways.

The straw that broke the camel's back and gave pause to their behaviour at the peak of the bullying was when they left racist and homophobic voicemails on my mum's answerphone.

Enough was enough. The school hadn't done anything to stop the bullies (with the exception of my amazing PSHE (Personal Health and Social Education) teacher), so my parents called the police. Thankfully, the police took the incident seriously. They traced the calls and offered to arrest those responsible. I didn't want any more attention and instead asked if the perpetrators could simply be cautioned.

I wasn't angry, I was just distraught and wanted the bullying to stop. My only hope was to be left alone so I could actually learn things at school, rather than finding opportunities to hide.

Neither did I hate the bullies. I hated myself for existing. I hated my face, my body, and I hated the fact that I was still breathing. I felt angry at myself for causing such behaviour in the bullies.

Whilst the bullying ceased, thanks to police intervention, my self-esteem plummeted.

I didn't know at that point that things were about to become much, much worse.

CHAPTER
FOUR

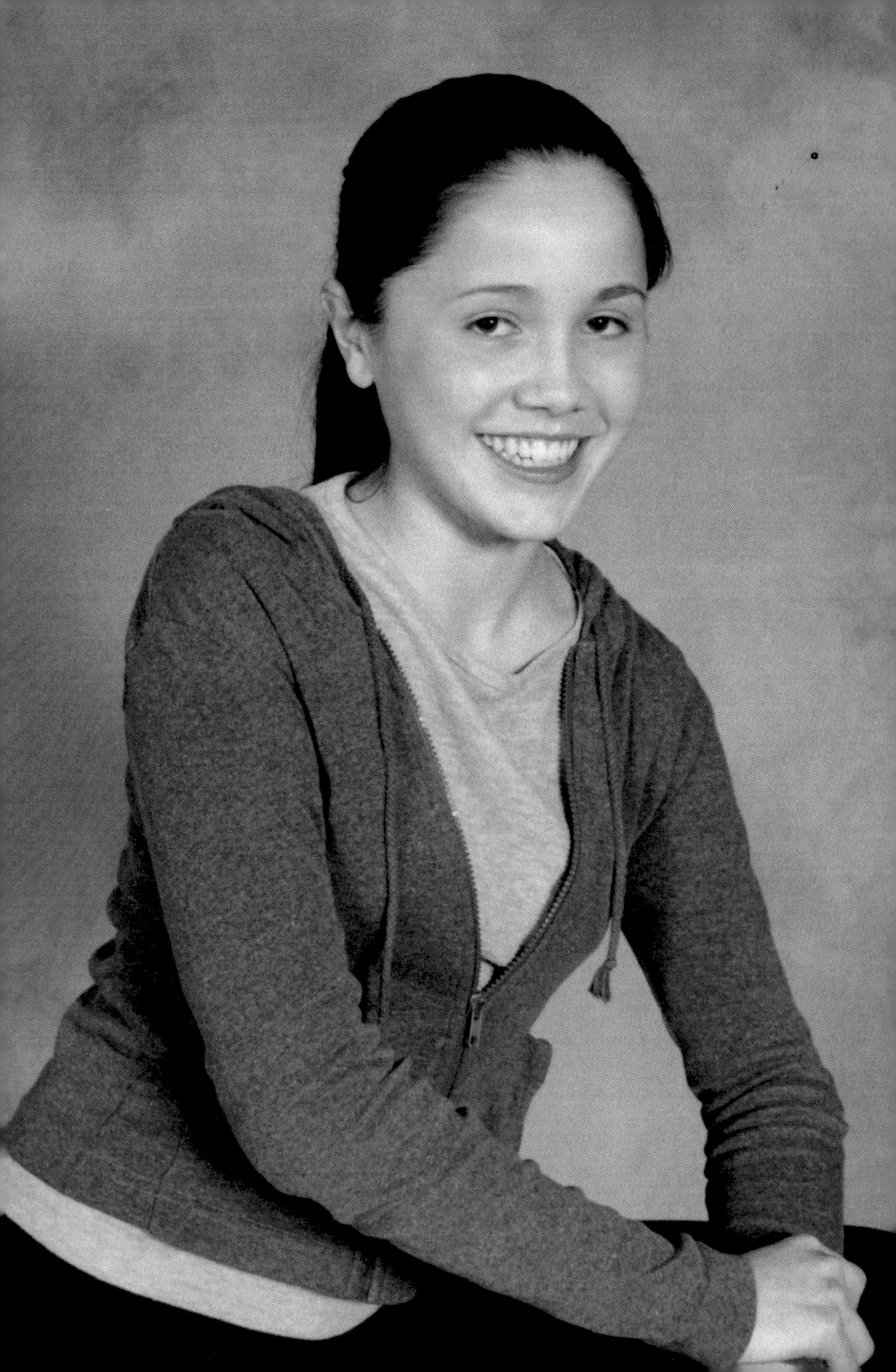

'Never be bullied into silence. Never allow yourself to be made a victim. Accept no one's definition of your life; define yourself.'
~ Harvey Fierstein

Oh, that bathroom! I'll never forget it. The dusky-pink bath and old toilet with a fluffy pink cover on its lid. The air reeking of bleach.

It could have been a bathroom in a nursing home, but it was in stark contrast to any home I'd ever been to. The lingering smell of bleach hid the stench of blood. It wasn't a safe haven for those in the twilight of their lives, but a place that stole the youth of those who passed through its doors.

A place where you were forced to prove your innocence.

Despite its promise of justice and respite, it was actually a gateway to Hell.

It was a safe house.

I'd been assaulted at a music festival and instantly whisked away, so that any evidence polluting my skin and insides was gathered and preserved. I was swabbed, prodded and questioned. A perfectly normal family weekend away, camping at a world music festival, had turned into a nightmare.

Following a forensic examination, where my young body was meticulously studied for any traces of my abuser, the staff suggested I had a bath.

I love a good soak, but as that dusky-pink bath lay before me... I couldn't bear the thought of removing the gown I'd been forced to wear. Revealing my dirty skin once again. But as warm water filled the tub, I knew I'd feel better if I immersed myself.

I took a deep breath and removed my gown. I dipped a toe into the lukewarm water and gradually lowered myself into the shallow depths.

It was a pitiful excuse for a wash. How could I be clean after what had just happened? Would I ever feel clean again?

That was the first time I self-harmed. It's a vivid memory.

I dug my nails deeply into my naked skin. I glanced around

for a bottle of bleach, or anything else I could use to destroy my dirty body and slaughtered insides.

That day, I lost my innocence. My childhood was ripped away from me. Even my clothes had been taken away and sealed in forensic bags. All that remained was a frail body, a broken heart, and that same ugly face I loathed.

As night began to fall, it was time to leave the safe house. I'd given video evidence, I'd been physically examined, and any item relating to the incident had been removed from me – other than myself. I couldn't help but wish my entire body had been sealed in one of those bags and sent away.

I didn't know how I'd cope with the pain and trauma – not only of that incident, but of the bullying, my low self-esteem, and my struggle to fit in.

We returned to the campsite. It felt odd revisiting the spot where my life, as I'd known it, had changed irrevocably just hours before. Though the perpetrator had been arrested and locked up, his tent was still there and his possessions.

Thousands of festival goers around us had no idea what had taken place as they carried on dancing into the early hours. I unzipped my tent and crawled into the confined space, then the smell of plastic overwhelmed me. Every single one of my senses had been polluted that day. I couldn't breathe. Whilst the assault hadn't taken place inside my tent, it was the same canvas that had shielded his abuse from the outside world.

I began to question myself: did it even happen? How could my life have changed so quickly? Why did we have to return to the place I'd been deeply traumatised and damaged forever?

I clung on to the fact that we were leaving the following day, returning north to where we lived. As soon as the sun rose and fellow campers began cooking their breakfasts, my family and I packed up the car.

We began our journey home. The nightmare was just beginning for me...I was about to lose all control of my life. My childhood was over – such things as arguing with my sister over sharing toys, of enjoying my favourite weekly magazine or devouring simple treats like Kinder eggs… My innocence had gone.

That was the first time a man touched me sexually. It wasn't just that it was unnatural…that man broke my soul. That moment saw me crash, unwillingly, into adulthood.

*

The minute we arrived home, I rushed to my bedroom. I needed some privacy. I huddled into a ball against my bedroom door, rocking backwards and forwards as I cried, 'Why me? Why me?'

It felt surreal. I could see my broken body from above; I thought I was watching someone in a soap opera as they coped with trauma…but it was me.

When a traumatic event occurs, it's often difficult for victims to accept normal life, despite this being what you crave. Everything seems ordinary, but you're painfully aware of how much your whole life has changed. Normality just serves as a cruel reminder of what once was.

I was still only thirteen. I had a boyfriend the same age; my friends and I went bowling then to McDonald's for a McFlurry. Now, all that felt empty. I felt tainted. Dirty.

I even wondered if I'd cheated on my boyfriend by being abused. How could I explain to my friends why I was now a shell of the person I was before?

I didn't look like a victim — if there even is a stereotype of a survivor of sexual abuse. Even after the assault, I wasn't timid. I didn't become a hater of men. In fact, I became the opposite.

I craved male attention and a desire to be loved — though I didn't want anyone touching me. Any physical pressure on my back was a definite trigger; it would bring flashbacks of my abuser's hands on my skin…he'd said he was giving me 'a full body massage'.

Before the incident, I'd wanted to save myself for someone special (like they did in rom-com movies). I'd imagined my first time would be with my first love, as part of a consensual relationship between childhood sweethearts. Now, I felt broken and dirty and, whilst I hated men touching me, I thought it better to let them do what they wanted, so that they wouldn't hurt me. I just wanted to be shown some affection, but to get that, I thought I had to sacrifice my body and soul.

Broken by that first attack, I thought I couldn't be broken any further. How wrong I was.

Transitioning into your teenage years is tricky enough, but coupled with trauma, these years were some of my toughest. Not only was I trying to discover my identity and place in the world, as well as coping with changes to my body, I was also battling flashbacks of the attack, self-esteem issues, and anxiety. Now I had to deal with 'grown up' stuff whilst still a child.

The attack itself didn't destroy me, what finally tipped me over the edge was the resulting court case.

I knew I had to give evidence because that was the right thing to do. I knew the attacker had a daughter the same age as me, and I knew I had to prevent him from doing the same thing to others.

I've always had a stubborn, determined side to me that has pushed me to keep going during the worst times of my life. I get particularly fired up if I see injustice in the world and I have a real desire to help others. What I struggle with, though, is helping myself.

I was lucky that, as part of the investigation, I had two police officers who believed in me and who encouraged me to go to court. Their care for me had a profound impact. I could tell they didn't judge me, my background, or that I lived in a poor suburb of Sheffield.

Despite their best efforts to look after me and my family, they couldn't protect me from the ordeal of going to court.

I imagine the wait for a court case is similar to the agony of awaiting medical test results. Your whole life feels on hold until you go to court. You do everything you can to go through the motions of everyday life whilst a grey cloud looms over you.

Before I got to court, it came out at school what had happened.

'You slag! No wonder someone abused you,' the bullies shouted.

There was even a bizarre air of jealousy, because I'd also hear, 'Why would someone want to abuse you?'

One day, when I was stood in the school dinner queue — which was a large thoroughfare in our busy state school — one of the bullies yelled, 'You deserve to be abused!'

All I wanted was to study at school. I had a drive to succeed and do well in my schoolwork, but my abuser's actions were now haunting me there, too.

I'd had enough. Though I'd rarely react or have the confidence to walk away when being bullied, I ran to the girls' toilets. I felt like a pinball, trapped in a game, as I pushed past the crowd of hecklers.

I quickly locked the cubicle door behind me.

I heard footsteps and I knew they'd followed me. They just wouldn't let me go.

I squatted on the floor inside the small cubicle and got the same whiff of bleach I'd smelled at the safe house. I wailed. I couldn't hold it in or hide it anymore. I tucked my head into my knees. Tears rolled down my face and dampened my clothes.

Why me? Why me? What had I done to deserve this? Was I really that bad a person?

I felt someone peering over me. I tilted my head and saw that one of the bullies had climbed onto the toilet next to mine and was now leaning over the cubicle.

'What's wrong with you?' she shouted.

I quickly stood up and unbolted the lock. I pushed past the other bullies congregating and ran into the corridor.

I'd always been well behaved at school. I was the one teachers put with the 'naughty kids' to be a good influence on them. I could always be found perfecting essays late into the evening and doing extra pieces of homework to impress my teachers. I even chose to spend my breaks in the medical room as I got on well with the school's nurse.

It was out of character, but I felt I had no choice. That day, I ran out of school. I just kept running. I had to get out of there.

The school was vast, unlike the confinement of a small, pop-up tent. The bullying had become just as suffocating; I may as well have been trapped in a small tent with the bullies, too.

I kept on running. The school was on the other side of the city to where I lived, and it took two buses to get home.

But how could I explain to my parents what was happening? They'd had to listen to details of my assault, and I wanted to protect both sets of parents from learning how bad things were for me at school.

I ran into Sheffield city centre. Shoppers casually walked past me, unaware of who I was or that I'd just run out of school. My heart pounded and my mind raced. I didn't want this life, this face, this body. I wanted to be someone else or just to die.

I went into Boots and bought a bottle of hair dye and boxes of paracetamol. Even if I were to die, I didn't want to look like I did, with my dark brown hair, chubby cheeks and broad body. I wanted to be invisible, even in death. I did not want to look the same as when I'd been assaulted.

I then made my way to a piercing and tattoo shop. At the secondary school I attended, we only had to wear uniform for P.E. classes, so I looked older than I actually was. I asked to have my belly button pierced.

As I lay in the chair, I glanced at the tattoo art on the walls and started to panic. The man who'd abused me had said he was a tattooist. He apparently did henna tattoos, which is how he'd lured me into his tent, with the promise of one.

'Ow!' The sharp needle piercing my skin brought me back to reality. It was done. I had a shiny belly-bar in my stomach, and I was a tiny step closer to being someone new. Someone different to that little girl in the tent who quietly whispered, 'No! I don't like it,' as my abuser made his way inside me.

The bullies didn't have control of me either. I was out of school. Then I felt a surge of anxiety…would I be in trouble? What would my parents say?

I rushed home. I wanted to get back before my sister finished school, and I still needed to dye my hair. I'd always felt proud to have 'virgin' hair; unlike many of my friends, I'd never dyed it. But given that my innocence had already been stolen, and in the worst possible way, what did a bit of hair colour matter?

To my relief, my parents were still at work when I arrived home. I went to the bathroom and began applying the hair colour. Whilst the colour developed, I took out the paracetamol I'd bought and went searching for more in the house. I pushed every tablet through its foil packaging and scooped them up before pouring a glass of water and going back to the bathroom.

I stared at myself in the mirror. My hair was matted with the dye and purple splodges trickled down my face. I clenched my fist to keep hold of all the tablets I'd gathered.

How had it come to this? My friends stressed over what we were doing in P.E.: netball or football. I wished I had such harmless worries; instead, I felt like the whole world was crashing down on me. I couldn't breathe.

My hand trembled as I lifted the tablets to my mouth. I was scared. I was so scared of dying. But I was also scared to continue living. My mental pain was so acute it felt physical.

I never meant to bring chaos and trauma to my family's door. I never meant to become a target for bullies and abusers. I figured it would be better for everyone if I was out of the picture. Then my family and friends could have a happy ever after — once I was no longer there.

My spiralling thoughts were interrupted when I heard my sister come through the front door. It brought me to my senses. I quickly threw the tablets into the toilet and flushed them away before she caught me.

*

When my case finally came to court, I had to return to the city where the assault had taken place to give evidence.

I took a train South with both sets of parents. I felt like I was the one about to face trial.

It was a busy train and I wondered what the other passengers would have thought if they knew what I was on my way to do.

I may not have looked like a broken, damaged little girl, but that's what I was.

I closed my eyes and pretended we were going on holiday. My dad had brought cheese sandwiches wrapped in foil — like when we went on road trips. I couldn't eat them. My body didn't deserve nourishment or comfort. It was dirty, and that dirt was about to be aired in public.

I squeezed my eyes shut and dug my fingernails into my arms. Why couldn't everyone on the train just shut up? How could they chatter about trivial things when I was about to relive a horrific nightmare?

I could hear my parents making small talk about the weather. However awkward that may have been, it wouldn't come close to hearing in court what happened to their youngest child.

It may seem strange, but I didn't hate my attacker. I wanted him to remain in custody, but only so he couldn't harm me or anyone else in the future. I began to imagine what he must be feeling. Did he care? Did he feel as awful as I did? Was he scared, too? I felt a pang of guilt for putting another human being through this torture. What if he hadn't meant it? What if he'd just had a moment of madness, and he was really a nice person?

That night we stayed at a Holiday Inn. Most other residents were there for business. We didn't know how long we'd be staying there; it depended on the case.

I was terrified of putting into words what had happened to me. I mostly blamed myself for the attack, but I also felt strongly about speaking out. I had to stop him from hurting others. As well as that, I couldn't face him being free to find me.

Whenever we'd stayed at a hotel, I'd always made the most of the cooked breakfast. That day, my stomach churned — scrambled eggs and unlimited toast and pastries did not appeal.

My life seemed worlds away to those of my peers. My friends were poring over maps in geography at school whilst I was miles from them, nervously awaiting my first experience of the UK justice system. They were learning about continents whilst

I put on a new shirt and black flared trousers, ready for the biggest day of my life.

My nightmare was about to become real. Professionals had promised me that this was the last hurdle to cross – then I'd be free to get my life back on track.

A taxi took us to Reading Crown Court. As we pulled up outside the courthouse, I noticed photographers everywhere, like paparazzi awaiting a celebrity. Were they there for me? Was the whole world going to find out about the disgusting things that had happened to me?

My parents tried to shield me as we got out of the taxi and the photographers started snapping away. Tears that had built up during the journey there began to fall from my eyes. I cowered in shock and my parents hurried me inside. I felt like those criminals on the news that had to be escorted and protected from the public as they went to and from their court appearances.

The clicking sounds from the cameras became distant. How did the press know that I was about to face the worst day of my life? How had they found out? Why were they so interested in getting photos of me and my family?

My thoughts urged me to run to the toilets for the opportunity to self-harm and release my tension, but my dad's voice to the court staff was louder; he demanded to know why the photographers had been allowed to take pictures of a minor – as a victim of a sex offence, he reminded them, I had a right to anonymity.

Apparently, the photographers were waiting for the high-profile perpetrator of another case; they were just taking shots of me in case we were linked.

We were seated upstairs in an area away from the main courtrooms. I had to give video evidence as I was too young to sit inside the actual court. It felt as if I was the one being locked away, unable to see 'justice' – whatever that looked like. Why were the general public allowed in the courtroom to witness the outcome of that terrible day, yet I had to sit it out?

I was comforted by Victim Support, who gave me a teddy bear with a slogan sewed on to the back: 'Good bears of the world'. It was a lovely gesture, but I couldn't appreciate a childish toy when I had to stand up like an adult against the man who had destroyed our family life as we knew it. Nevertheless, I wouldn't let it go.

The court process meant long periods of waiting, lots of conversations with big words, and numerous people nipping in and out of the room I'd been asked to stay in. The day passed and I didn't even get to give evidence. Back to the hotel to do it all over again the following day.

When, finally, it was my turn to speak, I was ushered into another small room with a TV screen, on which I could see the courtroom. There was a camera on me, so that the courtroom could see me, too.

Before the court case, I'd been given a book that outlined the procedure. It explained why barristers wore wigs (to show formality and solemnity; it wasn't to make you scared of them). It also described the justice system and what would be asked of me. It was helpful, but nothing could have prepared me for what I was about to endure.

I was asked a series of questions by my barrister; she was in her late thirties, friendly enough, but quite cold. I tried to focus on her eyes, but all I could think about was my parents in the courtroom, sitting amongst members of the public who wanted to hear my ordeal.

I dug my nails into my arm as I awkwardly answered her questions. Trying to recall what had happened in the lead up to the assault felt like an out of body experience. I could see myself hunched over a TV screen, my eyes looking downwards, watching as I tried to push out gross words about what that man had done to me.

I paused to take a sip of water. How I wished it was bleach. Why couldn't it contain something that could dissolve me from the inside out and take away the pain?

After a short break, it was time for the defence barrister to question me. Except, he didn't really question me...he just told me what he thought had happened.

His voice was stern. He looked straight at the camera; his eyes looked threatening on screen. I remember him shouting, 'I suggest you're lying! You're lying!'

Was this justice? The book never told me I'd be the one on trial.

I was back in a dark space with a man. But a different man this time. The barrister may not have been physically touching me, but he was attacking me.

I began to tremble. My body went into shutdown. Was I lying?

I'd always been told to listen to, and respect, people in power. But this man was so threatening, so cold. Was he lying?

The room began to spin. I tried so hard to focus on the screen.

'You're lying, aren't you?' he repeated.

I suddenly found my voice. 'No!' I wailed, 'you're lying.' Tears rolled down my face and I struggled to stay seated. I just wanted to crumple onto the floor.

The judge adjourned for a break and I asked to go to the toilet. As I locked the door behind me, I fell to the floor like a baby. I started to scratch at my arms then I pulled down my trousers to claw more deeply into my legs. I wished I'd brought some scissors to the courthouse. I couldn't bear the pain any longer.

I looked around for something I could use to hurt myself, but I couldn't see anything. I thought about wrapping the emergency cord around my neck, but I knew it would alert someone.

I felt trapped, like when I was in that dark, sweaty tent. I could feel the beads of sweat from my perpetrator's furrowed forehead drip onto my bare body.

I couldn't breathe. I felt just as vulnerable as when the assault had happened. My clothes from that day had been bagged up, shown in court, and endlessly scrutinised. It had been a sunny day and I'd worn a skirt and sequined bikini top, a typical festival outfit.

How had such an innocent break away with my family turned into this?

The court usher knocked on the door, bringing me back to the present, and the fact that I had to continue. I don't really remember what happened next.

I eventually left the evidence room and was taken to where my family was waiting. I remember seeing tears pour down my mum's face. My dad was as white as a sheet.

I remember us all hugging. And I remember sobbing and sobbing and sobbing.

*

With court finished for the day, we went to leave via the main entrance. At the bottom of the stairs was the defence barrister. Without thinking, I approached him and whispered, 'I'm sorry for shouting'. I felt ashamed that I'd lost control and raised my voice, when I tried to assure the court that I wasn't lying. Even at fourteen, I instinctively apologised for things outside my control.

I apologised to the man who, only minutes before, had broken me. A man paid tens of thousands of pounds each year to defend abusers. The man who had made me feel like I was the guilty one. I said sorry to him.

When back in court the next day that same man used my apology against me. He said I'd tried to sway the jury and the defence team — because some of them had seen me cry in the foyer.

Again, doubts started to creep in. Was I really that awful? Had I subconsciously tried to sway them? I just thought I was there to tell the truth.

Once I'd finished giving evidence it was time to go home. Was I now supposed to go back to Sheffield and to school as if nothing had happened? I was lucky that, whilst at school, I could confide in my form tutor, who was also my PSHE teacher. I stayed inside and helped her during break times, so that I didn't have to face the bullies in the busy corridors. She helped to keep me safe and distracted me whilst my fate was decided in Reading's courtrooms.

It was a tense time waiting for the police to call with the verdict. Every time the phone rang it felt as if an earthquake was rocking the house. The call eventually came, and I watched my mother's face drop.

What was it?

It was a hung jury—not enough jurors felt they could say that, beyond reasonable doubt, he was guilty.

I'd been through that terrifying experience for nothing.

Then other thoughts crept into my head. What if he found me? What if he did it again?

The two police officers who'd initially helped me visited. They felt they could get a guilty verdict in a retrial. They asked me if I would go through it all again.

I trusted them as they believed in me. I heard myself agreeing to a retrial. I had to do everything I could to prevent that man from harming others.

CHAPTER
FIVE

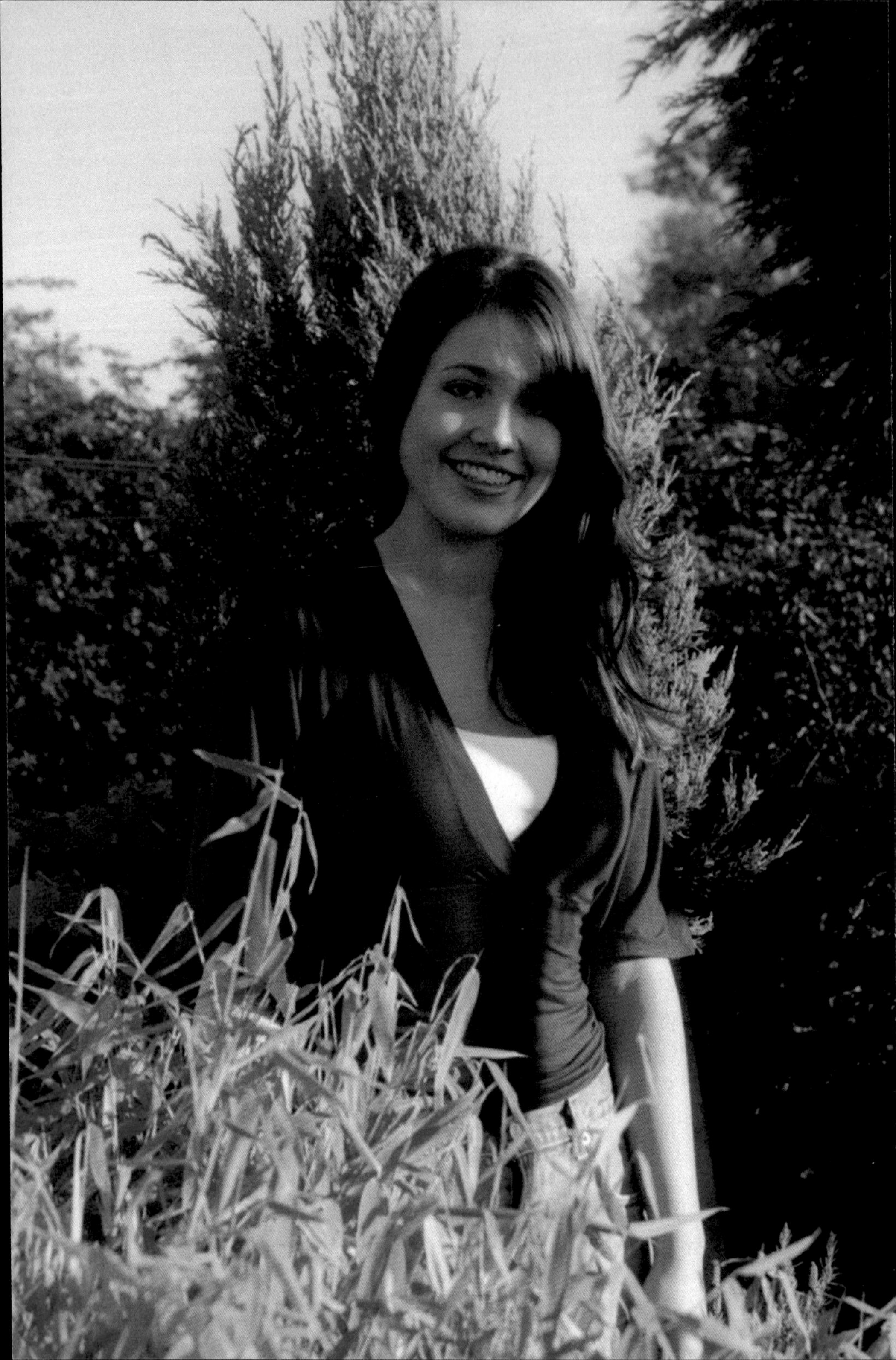

'Darkness cannot drive out darkness: only light can do that. Hate cannot drive out hate: only love can do that.'
~ Martin Luther King, Jr.

I'm not sure how I got through the following months, just waiting and waiting. Trying my best to be a normal teenager.

Going back to school. Swimming...bowling...the normal things teens do. But I wasn't myself, nor present in the moment. I felt like I wasn't in control of my own life. I was still trapped in our so-called justice system.

I tried to prepare myself emotionally for round two in court; I wasn't allowed any counselling until after the retrial.

I hated the uncertainty, the perpetual mental torture over what my future held.

Thankfully, I found some positive coping mechanisms. I didn't have to rely on self-harming as the only outlet for my worries and fears.

*

As I lay on my dad's living room floor, I felt sceptical. It was broad daylight and a kind woman I'd just met was trying to heal me with energy.

She asked me to close my eyes. A simple request, but something I struggled to do; it took me back to moments inside that tent when I lay helpless as I was abused.

There was something so calm and gentle about her that I felt at ease. I appreciated that someone had taken the time to try and help me. The woman was a friend of my dad's and a Reiki practitioner. She instilled in me some techniques to help me remain calm, for when I gave evidence at court a second time. Apparently, this had gone against me at the first trial, getting worked up.

Eyes closed, I could see glowing shades of orange and red. It felt as if the practitioner radiated heat from her hands. It was a nice sensation. All my stress and trauma reduced in that moment. Then I felt heat in my head, hips and knees.

When the session ended, she explained that her hands had moved over my body without touching it. She said she'd felt particular tension in my head, and that she'd detected warm parts in some of my joints, too, where I probably experienced niggling pain from time to time.

We had a few sessions together and she gave me a stone to hold for when I returned to court. The Reiki treatment gave me inner peace. A place inside of me that I could escape to whenever I felt overwhelmed by the outside world.

*

The time came to return to that small room within the court building. I clasped the stone tightly as the screen came on and I had to give my evidence. Instead of clawing at my arms I clenched the stone tighter and tighter to try and ground myself. This time, though I still shed tears as I recounted details of the assault, I remained calm. When the barrister tried to provoke me, I didn't react.

It was still a challenge, but so much easier than the time before. It was a different barrister, and I was also a different person.

Following the retrial, the jury's decision was unanimous. My abuser was found guilty. All the time, torture and turmoil that had gone into achieving that verdict culminated in tears of relief. I was neither pleased nor ecstatic, I was just relieved that I'd done something positive, which would hopefully prevent him from doing the same thing to another young person.

I hadn't 'won'. I wasn't victorious, I was a victim. I'd just survived the most gruelling of challenges. I can't say that justice was done, because the court process was, at times, worse than the abuse itself—a prolonged attack on my character, my identity and my right to speak.

At least now he'd be on a sex offenders' register; he had a criminal record and our efforts as a family had been worth it. I didn't know what his sentence would be, but I finally felt at peace. The truth had come out. I'd been believed.

I was finally able to access counselling at a specialist Rape and Sexual Abuse Centre near my home. I passed the centre every day on my way to school; little did I know that I'd be discreetly entering the place where so many women, men and children came after their hearts had been torn out — their sense of reality and perception of themselves altered forever.

The interior of the terrace-house-cum-counselling-centre was small and cosy. Yet it was still clinical, like the safe house had been. Staff dressed casually and, apart from some leaflets, it felt like a home from home.

At the centre I had sessions with a counsellor who was also an art therapist. We hit it off instantly. She was warm, down to earth, non-judgemental, and she just 'got' me. One day I noticed scars on her arm. They matched the scratches I had on mine.

Maybe I could be like her one day. Maybe I could recover. Maybe I could even use my experiences to help others.

Following the bullying and the assault, my self-harming had become much worse. I likened it to physically drawing out the pain I felt inside onto my skin. By now I was fifteen. I'd had my first boyfriend, I'd endured two court cases, and I was almost at the age of legal consent.

But my past haunted me and I couldn't stop poison coursing through my mind. I could not get the memory of the barrister shouting, 'You're lying, you're lying,' out of my head. I could not unhear the bullies and their taunts, 'Why would someone want to abuse an ugly bitch like you?' I could not 'un-feel' my abuser's hands creeping across my shoulders and under my bikini top. I could not forget that my first sexual experience had been with an abusive forty-two-year-old man, when I'd just turned thirteen.

I could not escape.

Digging knives and scissors into my body gave me a sense of freedom. In the moments when a blade cut through my skin, my internal pain evaporated. For a moment, my attacker's face faded from my mind. A blade cut through the bullies' words. As blood trickled out of my body, I felt free. Self-harming was something I could control. Nobody could take it away from me.

Nobody could ever hurt me more than I could hurt myself. I put the same stubbornness and strength that had helped me to survive into harming myself.

My counsellor understood this. She knew that she could not

simply throw away my knife. She could not lecture me about my misuse of scissors. She could not criticise my scars. All she could do was listen and understand.

She also knew that talking wasn't always enough. I'd experienced some horrendous things and I sometimes struggled to verbalise them.

Sometimes the pain I felt couldn't be put into words.

I'd been forced to talk about sex in court. Most families squirm when talking about the 'birds and the bees', but I'd had to describe, in intimate detail, what had happened to me – in public, and whilst my parents were listening in.

I didn't have to explain this to my counsellor. I didn't have to hide my scars or even show that I'd healed from my wounds. When I walked into that small room in that terraced house, I could just be me.

One day, my counsellor asked if I liked art. I said I didn't mind it, but that I wasn't very good. She explained that creative therapy could be an effective tool to help people communicate and express themselves.

In subsequent sessions we began to make a box to store all the things we'd talked about. She encouraged me to write a letter to my attacker, to explain to him how I felt about the incident.

I found it difficult, but in a good way. Writing down my thoughts helped me to focus my emotions. I put the letter in the box and imagined it would be collected by the postman, and that my attacker would receive it.

I drew a timeline of my life and included everything that had happened – good and bad. From memorable trips to Malaysia to see my family, to the bullying; from my parents splitting up, to the court case. It gave me some distance, as if those experiences had been someone else's, or that they were just ordinary, insignificant elements of my overall journey.

One day, during another art therapy session, I sculpted a knife from plasticine. Because I used knives to cut myself there was something symbolic about it. It also felt less of a secret, creating a tool I used to cope with everyday life. Except this knife couldn't hurt me. I shut it away in the box.

The therapy was a great distraction, and it also felt rewarding to create something than simply sitting and talking. I also started to write down my thoughts and feelings as another outlet; once my darkest thoughts were on paper, they didn't weigh so heavy on my mind. I placed anything I wanted to into the box I'd made, and it was shut away until the next session.

It didn't stop me from self-harming, but it did reduce the frequency, by distracting me whenever I felt the urge to cut myself.

Around this time, I discovered belly-dancing. I'd always felt too curvy for other dance classes. I loved the escape belly-dancing provided, and I dreamt of being a Hollywood actress. In such as ballet classes, I didn't fit in with the rich kids or the skinny girls — being curvy, mixed race, and living in the poorest part of the city.

The first time I saw belly-dancing off-screen was at a multicultural festival my mum had organised in our local park. I was drawn to the mirage of sequins, the whirls of colourful fabric and the sound of drums. A group of eight women, of all shapes, sizes and ages, twirled around with their gold canes. I loved the costumes, the music and the sheer happiness that radiated from them.

The women seemed to float along to the beat. They weren't stick thin like other dancers I'd seen, and yet they weren't the slightest bit bothered about their stomachs being on show.

I nervously waited until they'd finished their set and approached the group's leader. I asked how I could learn to belly-dance and she invited me along to their classes in a nearby church hall.

I learned to belly-dance with the same vigour and commitment I poured into my other obsessions. I went to every class. I saved my pocket money so that I could attend as many as possible.

Belly-dancing allowed me to lose myself in something much more positive and rewarding than creating scars on my arms.

CHAPTER SIX

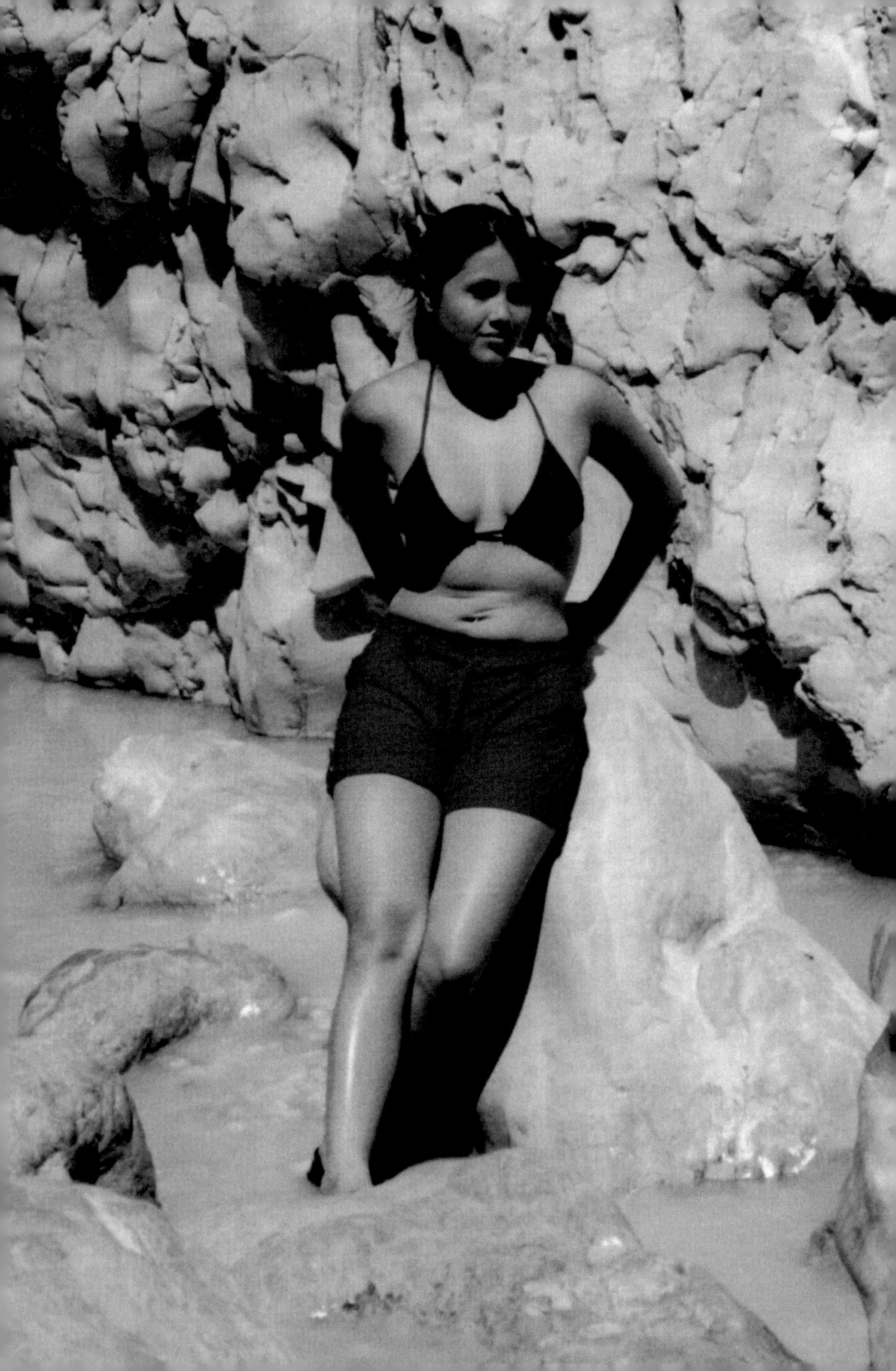

'Take your passion, and make it happen. Pictures come alive, you can dance right through your life.'
~ 'Flashdance' by Irene Cara

Enveloped by my heavy duvet, I flinched in pain as my craft scissors cut through the skin at the top of my thighs. Though my self-harming had subsided for a little while, the pressure of my upcoming G.C.S.E.s mounted. I was convinced I'd put on weight and the urge to cut myself reached a crescendo.

I was no longer a child; I was sixteen, and yet I still fostered habits I'd formed years before, such as cutting my skin and making myself sick.

I felt pathetic and embarrassed...disgusted with myself. I didn't just feel guilty about what I was doing, I felt shame, which is much worse.

It could be sweltering hot in our P.E. lessons as we ran around playing dodgeball, but I'd still keep my warm fleece sweatshirt on, the woolly material sticking to my bloodied arms. I couldn't risk people knowing what I was doing to myself.

I mostly cut the top of my thighs, so that my P.E. shorts covered my cuts. But, sometimes, when I really lost control, I'd cut any part of my body. In particular, I'd dream of slicing open my chubby cheeks and removing them altogether.

My counselling sessions had run out—there was no more funding to give me any further sessions than those allotted. I was on my own.

I was so focused on my G.C.S.E.s and determined to do well that I hardly allowed myself any time to go to belly-dancing classes. I gave myself no time to see friends, unless we planned to revise.

My G.C.S.E.s meant more to me than just exams—I told myself that they were my ultimate test. If I passed them, if I excelled in them, then I'd 'win'. I would have overcome my past challenges and I'd be victorious. Failure wasn't worth thinking about. If I failed, the bullies had won. If I failed, my abuser had won.

School gave us two weeks off to revise. A lot of my friends

slept in, socialised, and generally made the most of their free time. I set my alarm for 6 a.m. and I'd work solidly until bedtime. To keep me going, my daily nourishment was a bag of broken biscuits from the corner shop. I'd nibble on the biscuits whilst revising, as I tried to cram long notes into my head.

I had a strict revision method. I'd reproduce all my schoolwork, highlight specific elements, then write key points onto revision cards. I'd then turn the revision cards into mind maps. It was a long, arduous process, but I convinced myself that it was the only way I'd succeed.

I was stuck in my head, and my outlet became the bag of broken biscuits. But as I crammed more and more sugar into my mouth, I also felt a greater urge to purge. I felt guilty for consuming such junk, but it was the only thing that kept me alert enough to see my revision process through.

After I consumed each bag of biscuits, I rushed to the toilet and made myself sick. I thought I was managing my mix of addictions. I felt so much guilt if I digested the biscuits I'd eaten, but I also couldn't stop myself from eating the biscuits as this underpinned my revision process. It became a cycle I couldn't break.

As my therapy had finished, Mum invited a homoeopath to recommend natural remedies that would help me manage my stress, trauma and eating disorder. Though the sessions centred on alternative medicines and how they could help me with my issues, we also practised visualisation.

I remember one session where the homeopath asked me to picture a place where I could feel free. 'Close your eyes and relax,' she soothed. 'Imagine a place where you feel calm and tranquil. It might be a house, a beach, on a boat…it can be anywhere. Then think about what you're doing there… Are you sleeping? Dancing? Eating?

Her sessions were one of only two places where I felt I could relax—there, and whenever I was a passenger in a car. I struggled to sleep or feel settled anywhere else. As I shut my eyes, I tried to block out my attacker's face—this was always the image that came to me whenever my eyelids felt heavy. I focused instead on what the homeopath had asked me to visualise.

But I kept seeing his face. I kept feeling his hands on my shoulders. Those beads of sweat…

Eventually, his face began to fade, and I could see the tranquil beach of a desert island. I was there on my own, dressed in a yellow belly-dancing outfit, dancing with a silk veil. I was smiling. The sun was beating down on my face and I felt happy.

When the homeopath brought me back to the present, she suggested imagining this 'happy place' whenever I felt stressed or overwhelmed. The vision surprised me; I hadn't realised until that point just how much belly-dancing meant to me. It was also the first time I'd actually managed to push thoughts of my attacker from my mind.

*

As the build up to my exams mounted, I struggled to stay grounded and it was difficult to visualise. I forced myself to go to a few belly-dancing classes; although I found it hard to fully concentrate on the session, it was good to be away from my desk where my whole world revolved around passing my G.C.S.E.s.

By the time the exams came, I was exhausted. I hadn't wasted a minute on anything other than exam revision – even up to the moment I entered the exam room. I couldn't let myself or my family down. I had to succeed, I had to show myself and those who had supported me that my abuser had not stopped me achieving my goals.

No one had put any pressure on me – it was me that had set the bar so very high. I'd even opted to study thirteen G.C.S.E.s (including five languages), rather than the designated eleven.

Once the exams were over, I felt like I could breathe again. I went into party mode – not just for one night, for the whole summer.

My new crutch was alcohol. I'd drink to forget about the agonising wait for my exam results. I'd drink to make myself feel better about my fat face and my grotesque body. I'd drink because I wanted men to love me. I'd drink so my friends would like me. I'd drink to fit in.

Most of all, I'd drink to escape.

When I look back now, so many of my self-destructive cycles — whether over-studying or binge-drinking — stemmed from the fact that I hated myself. I gave myself unrealistic goals or forged unhelpful behaviours to either harm myself or make other people love me.

I didn't feel loved. I didn't love myself, and I was desperate to be saved from, or at least be free of, the pain I felt inside.

After a boozy, last minute holiday with my friend and her family, it was time to return home and open the dreaded envelope. My G.C.S.E. results had arrived.

I felt sick to my stomach. I ran to my attic bedroom. My hands shook as I slowly opened the envelope.

I quickly scanned the sheet and my heart leapt. I counted them up; I'd achieved six A*s, four As and three Bs. It was better than I could have dreamt.

I'd done it.

'Mum! Mum!'

She rushed upstairs. I shoved the piece of paper in front of her. She started to sob. I could only imagine how the previous few months must have been for her; I recalled her pale face after we stopped for her to retch in a field on the journey back from the safe house.

The incident was now a distant memory for both of us. That same child had just exceeded all expectations in her exams — despite two court cases, an eating disorder, torturous bullying, and a battle against self-harming.

Her tears turned to glee. We both leapt onto my bed and jumped up and down with joy. We then collapsed on each other, crying.

They may have only been exam results, but to me, they were a marker. I dread to think what would have happened had I not achieved them.

Perhaps, in a weird way, the assault was the driving force that made me succeed. Failure was not an option. It was all or nothing.

I put that same determination, effort, focus and emotion into my A Levels. I didn't link them to my attack in the same way, though I still put the same pressure on myself. I told myself that I needed those results to reach university and live a better life. I wanted to leave the area I'd grown up in. I wanted to be a success (I'd dreamed of being a barrister, but the court case destroyed all that).

I wasn't naturally academic. My plan was to go to college and study dance and drama — something practical, rather than stay at sixth form and slog away at academic subjects. As with anything I encountered — whether it was painful, gruelling or damaging for me — I put my full energy into it.

I revised as if I was reciting lines from a play. I even struggled to read my two A Level English Literature books: 'Harry Potter' and 'Tom Brown's School Days'. I couldn't concentrate or understand a lot of text all at once, so instead, I bought the revision guides for the two books. I didn't need to learn the content or enjoy reading it — I just needed to pass the exam.

As my focus was once again on exams, my eating disorder returned as the crutch that helped me to succeed. Only, this time, it became even worse. The bully inside me dominated my thoughts more and more over the years; now I had the pressure of exams again, she became both my best friend and my worst enemy.

I'd revise and snack, binge and purge, then revise some more. I became trapped in an insidious cycle: my 'crutch' started to control me, rather than me being able to control it.

My cheeks bloated from all the purging. My knuckles were sore from all the times my teeth had scraped against them as I bent over the toilet.

As well as revising, bingeing and purging, I'd go to work at the local supermarket. I put on some make-up and my uniform and I'd smile, hoping that nobody would detect the chaos I was living in behind closed doors. I worked long hours to pay for my belly-dance classes and various cosmetics.

I felt like a clown, buying even more make-up to cover my face. I worked with food all day but avoided eating at all costs in the hope I'd lose fat from my chubby cheeks (the irony is that bulimia actually causes bloated cheeks and glands, due to purging. It doesn't even get rid of many calories).

Bingeing then purging is not an effective method of losing weight. In fact, many people with bulimia gain weight over time. Your body starts to absorb calories the moment you put food in your mouth. If you vomit after a large meal, you typically eliminate less than fifty percent of the calories you've consumed. Laxatives will only rid you of a tenth of the calories you eat, and whilst purging may make you weigh less temporarily, this will most likely be water loss and not true weight loss.

Despite knowing all this, I still couldn't see sense. I didn't know how to work hard and consistently without my bulimia as a crutch. I was addicted to my eating disorder.

Work was a distraction, at least. Being stationed on the freezer section in the supermarket kept me fit, but I yearned to get home after each shift, so that I could return to my comforting binge and purge cycle.

My disorder remained hidden until my A Level exams loomed. Just as with my G.C.S.E.s, I put everything into each exam and would write line after line of text after each question on the test papers. I was purging in a different way — I had to 'get out' everything I'd ever learned. I had to get to the next stage: university.

I'd actually wanted to go to drama school, but that was too far away and too expensive; instead, I opted to study philosophy and Italian at the University of Manchester.

As the summer holidays arrived, with my exam results looming on the horizon, my eating disorder remained by my side.

One evening, as my stepdad drove me to my belly-dancing class, I broke down in tears. I explained how utterly exhausted I was. How tired I was of the bulimia. How tired I was of life.

My parents took me to see a doctor, who dutifully weighed me and recorded my measurements. 'Well, you look fit and healthy to me,' the doctor said. 'Your BMI is normal…a little on the upper end of normal, so you're fine.'

Fine?!

My whole life revolved around my addiction, yet my weight didn't reflect that of someone with an eating disorder. I felt ashamed. I was 'healthy'. There was just something wrong with me and who I was.

We sought the help of a local charity. They assured me that eating disorders are not defined by being underweight (a significant percentage of people with eating disorders would actually be classed as overweight).

After a long spell on their waiting list, I was invited to attend a group therapy session.

I was nervous about publicly admitting I had a problem; however, it was good to be surrounded by people who also struggled with weird habits around food. I was surprised to find 'normal' people with similar issues to me in the group. I couldn't help but giggle when it came to break time, when the group leader sheepishly offered tea and biscuits to us all.

In these sessions we looked at recovery, and ways to better manage our eating disorders.

I never said it aloud, but I didn't want to recover. My disorder was the only thing in my life I could rely on. I couldn't fool the group leader…one day he took me aside and said, 'You're going to get worse. I don't think you're ready for this yet.'

I was devastated. How could it get any worse? I wanted to live a life without my eating disorder, but at the same time, I wasn't ready to let go of it. It was a vicious cycle of self-destruction, both mentally and physically.

The only time I relaxed a little was when my stepdad drove me to and from dance classes. It was the only time I allowed myself to rest.

After spending some time on a different waiting list, I was able to book a few aromatherapy sessions. My old fears resurfaced, and I was worried about someone touching me. I was also scared to allow myself time for the therapy out of my chaotic schedule.

Following an initial consultation, I laid on the massage bed. The special blend of essential oils helped me to relax. The glands in my throat felt sore as I placed my puffy face into the hole of the bed.

What felt like only minutes later, I felt a gentle rock on my shoulders. 'Are you okay?' asked the therapist gently. 'I think you drifted off. You probably needed it.'

She was right. I'd not let go for a very long time.

I felt a pang of guilt. I wasn't worthy of a rest. I wasn't worthy of someone looking after me.

But it felt so nice to take a break from the bulimia. In the car journey home, my mum was eager to hear about the session, but I just closed my eyes and slept. The aromatherapy oils were still soaking into my skin, and I managed to dream—rather than just collapsing into bed through exhaustion in the early hours of the morning.

*

A Level results day. I eagerly checked online to see if I had an offer from the University of Manchester.

I'd got a place! I managed to achieve two As and two Bs, which was more than enough to get me into university.

I didn't feel the same excitement as I had when receiving my G.C.S.E. results. I just felt relieved and exhausted.

I later found out that I'd achieved 100% marks in my English Language and Literature A Level exam. I hadn't even read the books; it was only through my gruelling revision regime that I'd managed to pass with flying colours. I didn't feel that I'd learnt anything, I'd just trained to pass the exam.

Setting the bar so high meant revising for exams took over my life, my health and my mind. Maybe I could achieve anything I wanted to—but at what cost?

CHAPTER SEVEN

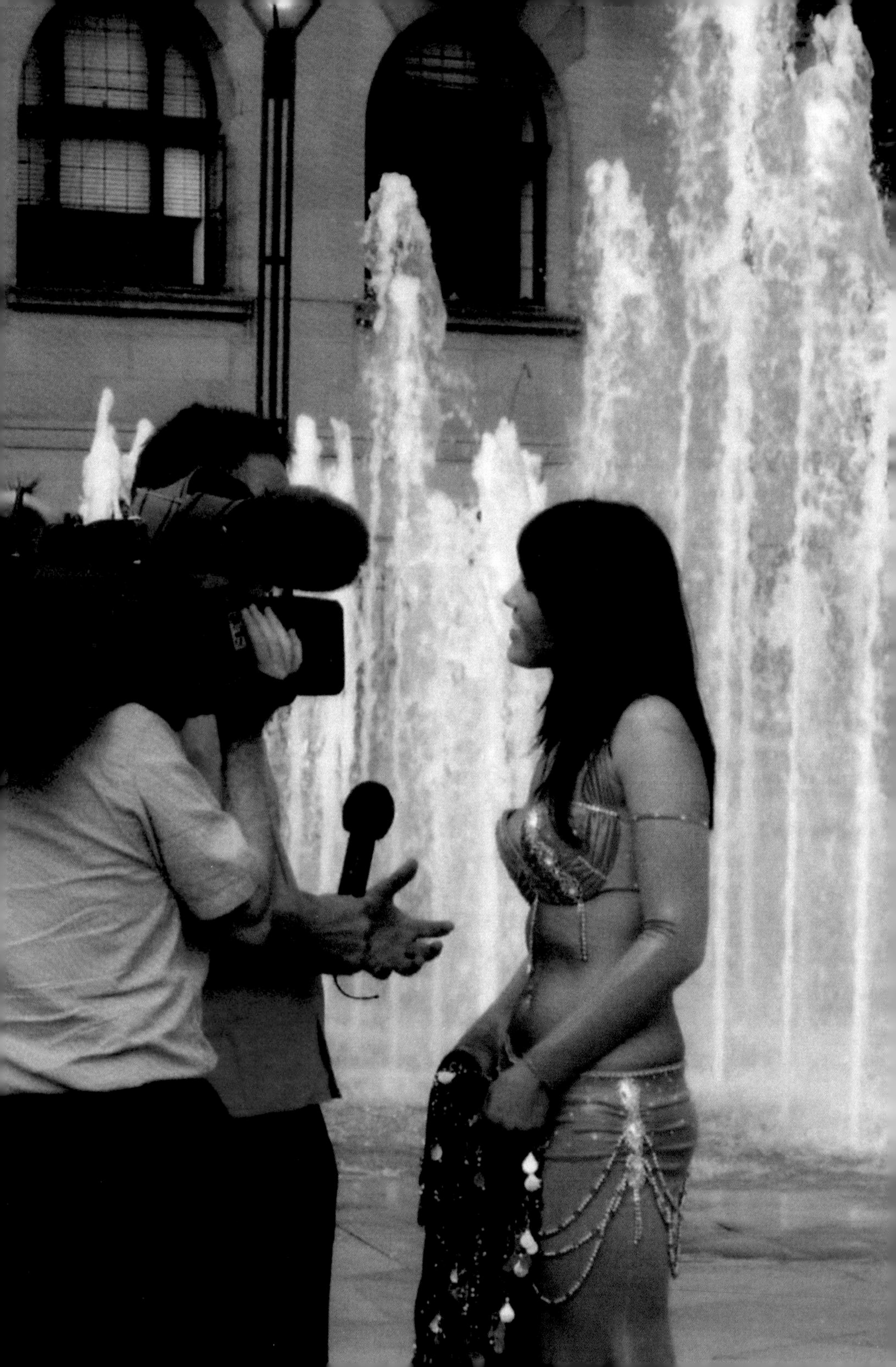

'You've gotta dance like there's nobody watching, Love like you'll never be hurt, Sing like there's nobody listening, And live like it's heaven on Earth.' ~ William W. Purkey

It was soon time to face my next challenge: moving to Manchester for university.

I worked at the supermarket up until moving day. My parents had helped me buy every possible item I needed in pink — I had it in my head that all my utensils, everything, had to be perfect and pink.

As I nervously laid out my possessions inside the small box room I'd been assigned in the university's halls, I felt a wave of hope. Perhaps this was the fresh start I needed. Perhaps this would help me with my issues and give me a new future.

I threw myself into freshers' week. I was party girl, binge drinker, socialite, and the one who made a fool out of herself. After each night of 'fun' and escapism came a day of anxiety, regret and an overwhelming feeling of isolation.

I didn't know how to be comfortable in my own skin. I'd overanalyse every conversation I had. I'd think back to the night before and hate myself for being louder than everyone else. I would never get angry at anyone other than myself.

I hated being so ugly and hated that my self-hatred had followed me to university. It dawned on me that I was still the same person, just in a different location.

At uni, I couldn't escape things like I could at home. I had a small room in an apartment with twelve other people. I had to share a bathroom, so I couldn't ease my anxiety by making myself sick. I felt such strong urges to binge and purge, but I couldn't. No one could know my dirty secret.

Once lectures kicked in, my days had a rough structure, which helped a little. But I struggled with academia. Now I was amongst other high achievers, I couldn't fake it anymore. I was exhausted from trying to fit in all the time.

As a distraction, I threw myself into my extracurricular activities. I joined every society going; I also found belly-dancing classes in Manchester. I attended youth theatre, and I began looking for a job.

As my agent was based in the area, I got work as a belly-dancer throughout Greater Manchester.

I applied for jobs in catering and did some silver service waitressing. I also got a job in the food court of Selfridges. It was ironic that my work revolved around food and drink.

My passion for dance and drama helped me escape or avoid the academic studies I had to endure in my lectures. I didn't fit in with most people I encountered at university; they were well spoken, naturally gifted at academia, and most were quite pompous (especially those in my philosophy lectures).

I'd work all day then dance at night. Somewhere in-between I'd also cram in drama classes and social activities. After a while, I became wholly focused on dancing and auditioned for shows all over the country.

I successfully auditioned for a new BBC dance show and made it to the quarter-finals. I danced in a Bollywood theatre show in Leeds. I began to neglect my university studies; all my energy and focus went into dancing and performing.

I have an all or nothing personality. Dance became my absolute 'all' and university got 'nothing.'

I would dance hard and party hard then start all over again. I'd rarely make it back to the halls of residence. I remained committed to my dance and drama, regardless of how well I felt; my studies felt like my nemesis — they were the distraction now.

During my second year of university, I saw an advert for an ITV show called Britain's Got Talent. I applied and got called to audition with producers.

I'd attended all sorts of auditions by that point and was often waved away when the casting people learned that I didn't do traditional ballet, tap or jazz. This audition was different. They seemed to love that I was there in my belly-dancing outfit and that I wasn't delivering a traditional performance. I may not be the best dancer, technically, but I do know how to put on a show. Whenever I dance, I'm someone else, someone much happier and more confident than insecure Sophie. I come alive when I dance.

One night, whilst watching Manchester United play on TV, I received a phone call. It was a producer from the show.

'We've got some good news. You've made it through to the live auditions. You'll be performing in front of three judges: Simon Cowell, Piers Morgan and Amanda Holden.'

I couldn't believe it! Failed auditions and the dance troupes I couldn't get into had knocked my confidence, yet I'd been successful in the biggest audition of my life. I'd not even seen the show before — that night I jumped onto YouTube and watched the entire first series.

My stomach lurched when talented performers were slated by the judges. I'd only ever performed in restaurants on my own, or at community festivals as part of a belly-dancing group, and now I was going to perform on live TV.

I only told my housemates that I'd been invited to audition, as I didn't want to place too much pressure on myself. I had private belly-dance classes with my agent in preparation…I only had a minute and fifteen seconds to impress the judges.

A space in my bedroom, measuring approximately a square metre wide, was where I practised. I imagined it was the huge stage in the theatre rather than the only uncluttered spot I had access to amid the uni halls. Unsurprisingly, my whole focus became the audition. I saw it as my one opportunity to make it as a performer and live my true dream.

A few of my housemates accompanied me to the audition, which was held at the theatre on Oxford Road, Manchester. We queued up outside, along with clowns, street dancers, drag queens, singers and impersonators. And there I was, in my belly-dancing costume.

As we had a long wait ahead, my housemates bought cookies from the supermarket opposite. We stood munching them in the cold for almost two hours.

I didn't really know what to expect from the experience. Everything felt surreal. Inside, we had an even longer wait, but we made friends and chatted to the other acts. The production team was lovely and made us feel at ease.

Eventually, I was directed to the edge of the stage, behind the curtains. I was petrified; the sound of the buzzers was deafening when the judges didn't like an act. As I warmed up, Ant and Dec came over with the camera crew. They were so warm and friendly.

My turn came. I was told to walk to the star on the stage, where the spotlight pointed, in front of the audience in the packed theatre.

It was far removed from shimmying around a local restaurant. My nerves were rife. I was about to perform in front of a thousand people – three of whom, on a platform at the front, were renowned for being brutal with their comments.

Once I stood on the star, the crowd cheered. Ant and Dec were egging me on in the wings and even Simon Cowell smiled at me.

I quietly introduced myself and the audience clapped. Once the music started, though, I went into my 'dance trance'. I put all my nervous energy into feeling the music.

No buzzers drowned out my song and I was left to wriggle and shimmy away. The song ended and I became quiet, coy Sophie again. I relaxed from my end pose and stood up, my shoulders automatically hunching over.

'Your wiggle or wobble, whatever you call it,' said Piers, 'is really good. You've got a great belly for belly-dancing. I thought it was bloody marvellous!'

Amanda loved my performance and so did Simon, who said, 'You've got a definite yes from me.'

I couldn't believe it – they all said yes! I walked into the arms of Ant and Dec who celebrated with me. We all jumped up and down with joy. Prima ballerinas had auditioned but not been successful, then there was me – a far cry from a typical dancer or stage school graduate.

That night my friends and I celebrated in our student digs with a bottle of cava and a Chinese takeaway.

But would I make it to the live semi-finals? I was asked to travel to London's West End, where I'd be told in front of the cameras whether I'd got through.

One of my dreams was to perform in the West End. I'd paid to attend a few drama and dance workshops in London, but I'd never thought that someone like me would be on that stage.

Again, there was a lot of waiting around and interviews to record before we found out who was going further in the competition and who would be going home disappointed. I was put with a small group of fellow performers and we were soon next to get our decision. Waiting on the steps leading to the stage I got chatting to a drag act called Tracey and we hit it off straightaway. We linked arms as we made our way on stage to face the judges.

'Well, I'm sorry to say…,' Simon began. We all froze, ready for the blow. '…you've made it through to the live semi-finals!'

I couldn't believe it! I leapt for joy and grasped Tracey's hands. I'd been fully prepared to hear that I hadn't made it to the semi-finals; I'd even gone with that mindset. There were so many talented acts and I believed I fell short. But, for the first time, not being traditionally trained and not embodying a typical dancer seemed like a real gift — something rare and precious I had to make the most of. Life was about to change for the better — I had to seize this opportunity.

Everything else went out of the window. I did the bare minimum in my university studies, I cut out any socialising — and I just about managed to continue my shifts as a waitress, which paid for my dance tuition.

I couldn't tell anyone and tried to carry on as normal. Every spare moment I spent rehearsing in the little space in my bedroom. I even hired a small community space, so that I could practise with the props I would use on the show.

Nobody knew it, but it felt like my dreams were coming true. All those years of dance classes, drama tuition and throwing myself into random performances of any kind had come to this.

Eventually, my first audition in front of the judges was aired. My flatmates and I gathered round an old TV in the shared lounge of my student digs. It felt amazing as they all cheered me on, but all I could focus on was how chubby I looked on screen.

Was I really that ugly?! Did I actually look that curvy?!

My audition even made the newspapers. I couldn't get over it: little Sophie Mei, with her flabby belly and imperfect moves, had been splashed all over the nationals. I bought three copies of each newspaper as souvenir keepsakes.

My phone started buzzing. At first, it was just excited friends and family, then I began to receive calls from journalists who wanted to set up interviews and photoshoots.

I needed to get myself in the best shape possible for the live semi-finals and the press attention. I got up at 6 a.m. every morning and went for a run. I cut all carbs from my diet. I'd rehearse for a few hours each day in my room, attend a dance class, then go to the gym whenever I was free. I listened to the song I'd chosen for my performance in the live show over and over and over again.

When I had to go to my job as a waitress, I'd visualise dancing on the show in front of ten million people.

It was intense and also quite lonely, as a solo performer rehearsing on my own.

I was relieved to meet with the producers. They said backing dancers would accompany me during my performance. Lots of muscly, half-clothed men. Though this would undoubtedly excite a lot of people, I felt intimidated. On stage I oozed confidence, but behind closed doors I was a confirmed introvert.

I rehearsed with the backing dancers as well as a professional choreographer who taught people on BBC's Strictly Come Dancing. I felt way out of my depth and wondered at what point they'd find out I wasn't a 'proper' dancer…that I was simply an ordinary person, an imposter, living their dream.

I wasn't outed. People said it was refreshing that I'd just rocked up as I was. Naive but passionate.

I remember going for costume and make-up practice and the professionals couldn't believe that I'd never used hair extensions or applied false nails. I thought putting on eyeliner was a good effort.

They transformed me from an ordinary waitress into a superstar diva (without the attitude). Everyone behind the scenes appreciated that I was just 'me'.

As the semi-finals loomed, I cut more and more from my diet. I'd seen so much interest in — and bullying over — my curvy body that I felt I had to resolve the issue for the next round.

I couldn't win. Some women loved me for 'championing curves' whilst others said I was grotesque. Any focus on my body, good or bad, made me scrutinise it.

I quickly learnt to ignore online comments; none were particularly helpful, and the nasty ones lingered the most.

Nothing was going to stop me from giving my best performance. I worked hard and the show was my only focus. I barely ate a thing the day before; instead, I rehearsed and rehearsed and only broke off to use the hotel's sunbed.

There was a dress rehearsal on the day of the show. The stage didn't seem as big as I'd feared nor the size of the auditorium, which brought some relief.

Moments before I went into hair and make-up, production told me that my music had been re-edited. I started to cry. I'd rehearsed to the same beats for months. And now, just a few hours before the biggest performance of my life, I had to relearn parts of the song and the dance routine that had become second nature.

Everyone backstage was supportive and they helped me get back in the zone. That's live TV — anything can change right up until the moment it airs.

My make-up was applied, and my hair curled and volumised. A screen backstage showed the auditorium and the judges. In my mind, I could see my family, my dance teacher and my friends watching, and I shuddered with nerves.

We queued up to perform. As I watched the routines before mine, I panicked — the judges weren't holding back with their critiques. This was either going to be the worst thing that had happened to me or the best.

My turn came.

I waited in position behind the stage doors whilst my VT footage had played, which showed my journey to that point from my initial audition. I tried to embody my favourite Hollywood stars who oozed confidence and sex appeal.

The doors opened, the smoke machine whirred into life, and my track began to play. I gave my best performance and danced around the stage. At one point, my ankle caved, but nobody seemed to notice.

I made it to my end position — my signature back-bend pose — without hearing any buzzers or booing from the crowd. All I heard was lots of cheers.

I had to stand for the judges' reactions. Huddled next to Ant and Dec, I went from confident performer back to shy student.

I felt more pressure this time, as I understood what a big deal this was.

Piers said, 'It's been emotional watching you. That was exceptionally charming.'

Amanda, a big supporter of mine and everything I stood for, said, 'You win. You so win, lady. You look beautiful. You're sex on legs. That performance was absolutely knock out. Well done!'

Then Simon gave his verdict. 'Let me tell you, Sophie, this is what this show is all about. I thought that was fantastic. Absolute star quality. Massive improvement from when we first saw you. And you look incredible tonight. I thought that was terrific. Congratulations!'

Had I heard them correctly? I was speechless. I literally skipped off stage, desperate to hug my family.

Getting further in the competition came down to a public vote, and this time I was right to assume I wouldn't make it through. Whilst I was slightly disappointed, I was also relieved that this once in a lifetime opportunity had ended on a high.

Backstage, I sought out Amanda and Simon to thank them. We chatted easily, discussing the X-Factor. Simon was lovely; I genuinely believe that he likes to see good people do well. 'You could take that performance anywhere in the world,' he said.

I couldn't believe how positive and supportive everyone was

being about me! It felt incredible.

The next day, I was all over the press again and interviewed by Eamonn Holmes on This Morning.

Whilst I received some criticism over my weight, most feedback was positive. People asked, 'What have you done to get those abs?'

It was difficult returning to normality. That said, my summer was already booked up, with gigs across the country following my appearance on the show.

The constant dancing began to take its toll. Performing daily, constantly putting on costumes and applying make-up, and trying to please large audiences, was amazing but incredibly draining. I struggled; my adrenaline peaked and troughed, and I became even more disciplined over what I ate. My career may have been booming but things felt out of my control.

I turned to my crutch...and controlling what I could control. Food.

I'd already lost weight due to my punishing dance schedule — enough that my friends and family became concerned.

It was agreed that I'd return to my studies. As part of my degree, I was to live in Naples for a year, from September. My interview with a dance, drama and English school called La Fabbrica Del Divertimento (the Fun Factory) — a small school on Mount Vesuvius — was successful.

I think my loved ones assumed that a break from dancing would help with my appetite — especially as I'd be in Napoli, the home of pizza.

Was that all it would take? Would living in a land famed for pizza, pasta and good wine solve my fear of consuming carbs?

CHAPTER
EIGHT

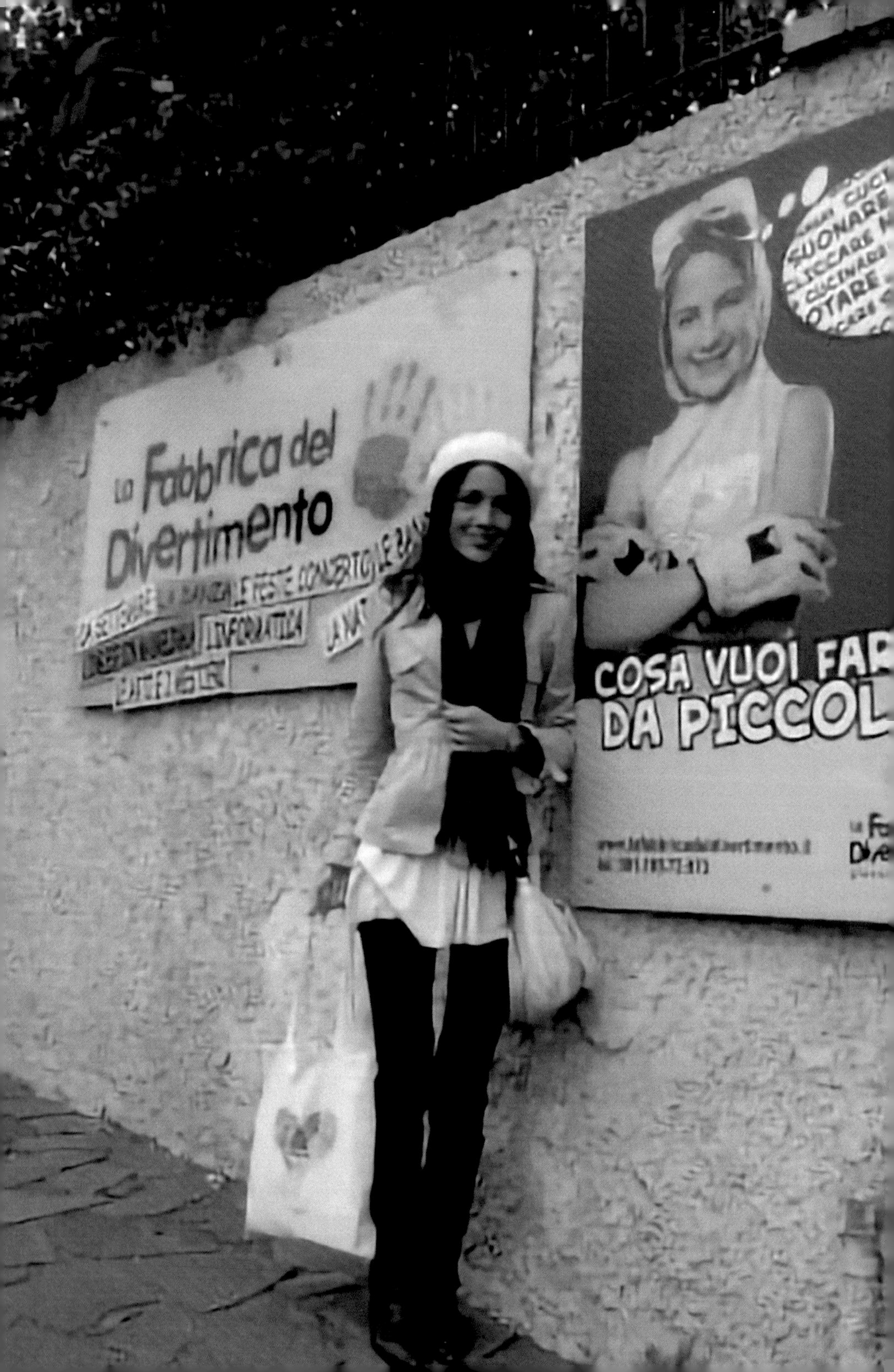
La Fabbrica del Divertimento
SUONARE
COSA VUOI FAR
DA PICCOL

'There was never a genius without a tincture of madness.'
~ Aristotle

Making my way up the stone steps I came to what looked like the entrance to a prison cell.

Was this really where I would be living during my year abroad?

After several minutes, I managed to manoeuvre the key into lock and twist it.

The hallway hadn't done my new abode justice at all. I felt like I'd walked onto the set of an old Italian movie. My apartment came complete with a balcony that overlooked Mount Vesuvius.

The only downside was that I had to share it with another English teacher.

I'd become used to having my own room and eating area, where I could practise as many weird habits as I liked.

I'd shared a kitchen and bathroom at university, so I tried not to feel too perturbed. After all, this was my fresh start. A break from the pressure of my dance career and time out of the 'spotlight', so to speak.

What I hadn't realised then is that your problems follow you. And that, sometimes, change can make things much, much worse.

I threw myself into learning Italian, and teaching English through dance and drama, with some of the most beautiful human beings I've ever met.

I tried to immerse myself into Napolitan life and, whilst I tried to be proactive and sociable, I had to also face my worst fears: meals out and meals in groups, with predominantly carbohydrate-based dishes on offer.

Of course I was going to find it hard. Lunch and dinner were shared affairs. I had to learn how to control such situations.

To excuse my refusal to eat carbs, I learnt how to say 'I have a gluten intolerance' in Italian. I was already a vegetarian, which also helped me avoid a lot of other foods.

But I needed more excuses, more methods, to avoid carbs.

I ate salads and small portions of buffalo mozzarella — another speciality of the area. I drank espresso to keep my energy up and, whenever I had the chance, I opted to cook for myself. I'd make salads from leaves, carrots and cucumber, or vegetable soups with just a stock cube for flavour. I rationed my fruit and only ate half an apple a day. I ate only the whites of eggs.

From all the running around, teaching and socialising, and with such a limited diet, I was exhausted. My body became frail. A cold breeze felt like lots of small knives prodding at me.

I replaced my food intake wherever possible with espresso. I turned down offers of wine and drank fizzy water instead, to keep me full. Every meal became a battle. My head told me to avoid food at all costs, whereas my heart wanted to spend time with the families I'd got to know. I hated appearing rude and shunning food, but I couldn't allow myself to slip. I could barely concentrate on what people were saying when I agreed to the offer of dinner.

Inevitably, the more food I ate from my 'off limits' list, the more I had to make my excuses and run to the bathroom to make myself sick.

I couldn't allow any calories to linger in my body. I genuinely felt like all carbohydrates were there to attack me, and those encouraging me to eat them were trying to kill me.

Carbs were the enemy and I had to fight them off at all costs.

When I felt weak my habits became even more bizarre. I spotted some chocolate in the fridge I shared with my roommate in our apartment — a large pack of Dairy Milk minis. I can still remember that packet; it was half open and staring at me.

I was working on a university essay about my experiences in Italy. I allowed myself one Dairy Milk chocolate. The sugar kick struck me like a lottery win, but after a few moments, feelings of guilt and shame kicked in.

I had to get the evil entity out of my body, but to make myself sick I needed more food and more fluid. I devoured the rest of the chocolate like I hadn't eaten for weeks, downing as much water as I could.

It didn't take long to fill my shrivelled stomach and I rushed to the bathroom. I switched on the shower in case my flatmate returned, bent over the toilet, and scratched my long nails down my throat. I had to get rid of the evil poison I'd put in my body.

I retched, but nothing came up. I pushed my fingers further down my throat—my teeth cut into my knuckles, drawing blood. I kept pushing until I retched again. I managed to vomit a little, but it wasn't enough.

After twenty agonising minutes I'd expelled what I could from my body. My cheeks were puffy, my eyes, bloodshot, and my hands, sore. It didn't matter to me...I'd have drunk bleach to get the chocolate out of my system.

I turned off the shower and cleaned up the vomit and blood from in and around the toilet bowl.

What was I doing? How had it come to this?

I vowed never to touch my roommate's chocolate again. But I still yearned for a sugar kick. A bit of indulgence...I even craved making myself sick and the feeling of relief when I'd managed to vomit.

It's difficult to describe, but whilst making myself sick was extremely painful, it also felt rewarding. I thought I was in control, but I was actually locked in the binge and purge cycle—which can feel much worse, much dirtier and is much more hidden than anorexia. I felt like a drug addict who'd got her fix. But what if I hadn't managed to get rid of it all? I couldn't live with residue calories in my body, poisoning me.

I decided that the best option was laxatives, so I went to the local pharmacy to buy a few packets. I lived in a small village with just a few shops, so I had to be careful not to look like I was doing anything abnormal.

I rushed back to the apartment and took around twelve laxatives. I couldn't wait for them to work, but neither could I purge anymore; the laxatives would come up, too, and I didn't want to waste them.

So began my addiction to laxatives. I went to a different store each day to buy them and it wasn't long before I increased the amount I took. I longed to relieve my body of any food or fluid I'd consumed. As soon as I ate or drank anything, I wanted it out.

The winter months kicked in and I increasingly felt the wind sharpen its blades against my skin. I had to wear layer upon layer to cope with the cold.

My periods stopped and I had no sex drive; I'd finished with my boyfriend back home in the UK anyway. I needed to focus on what was in my control—my body. If anyone tried to criticise or feed me, I'd scream to myself for them to leave me alone.

I still craved male attention. I met the security guard of a local museum on one of my lunch breaks (I often went out at lunchtime, to avoid eating with my colleagues). I'm not sure that I fancied him, but he gave me the attention I desired. I didn't always understand him either, as he spoke only Napolitan (an Italian dialect).

He invited me over to his apartment—he wanted to cook dinner for me. His small flat was bare, apart from a solitary table and chairs, a computer, and baseball bats. He began to talk about some of the bats; I assumed he was interested in the sport or a collector of baseball memorabilia.

I thought it was nice that he was sporty, that is, until I realised what he was saying…the bats were ones he used to attack football fans. He was part of a hooligan football group.

I thought we shared a love of football, but it was actually an outlet for his anger and hatred.

I felt sorry for him. He lived alone, in an impoverished place, and he'd lost his mum at a young age. The trauma he'd experienced had radicalised him to hate others, whereas my trauma had encouraged a hatred of myself.

I wanted to leave his flat, but I was trapped, and I didn't want to cause a scene or be rude. Worst still, he'd made pasta. I would rather he hit me with one of his baseball bats than force me to eat macaroni cheese.

I played along so I could get out of there, but I did not want to eat at any cost. Ironically, as a kid, macaroni cheese had been my favourite comfort food; now, it was poison.

What if he killed me? My thoughts strayed to my parents, friends and colleagues…how angry they'd be that I'd willingly gone with a stranger to his apartment. All those warnings as a kid and here I was, aged twenty, in a stranger's home, and I hadn't told anyone.

He laid out dinner and ushered me to sit down and eat. I asked for a drink and when his back was turned, I quickly hid some of the pasta in my bag, so it would look like I'd eaten it. 'Buonissimo,' I declared when he came back with the glass of water.

After a few mouthfuls, I persuaded him to take me out — to see some of Naples' sights by night. That way, we'd be in public. More importantly, I could avoid the food.

When I finally got to my apartment that night, I ran up the steps and hurriedly wiggled my key into the stiff lock to get inside.

I'd survived.

The next day I confided in my bosses, who'd become friends, about who I'd been with the previous night. They were mortified and explained how dangerous some of the hooligan group were.

I hadn't seen his violent side, only the lonely, depressed, impoverished person he'd become. I wanted to help him, but my bosses made me promise not to see him again.

I wanted to be loved, even if that love came from the wrong people.

*

A lot of male friends I'd made since being in Italy said I was too skinny, and that I needed to put on weight. They added that Italian men loved 'meat on their women'. But I'd started to see each of my ribs, and I loved that my thighs had almost wasted away to the bone.

I'd grab any fat still clinging to my body and wish it away. I tried to be even stricter with my diet and added more exercise into my day. I wouldn't let anyone stand in my way.

In my head, I was not too skinny or skeletal at all; I finally felt successful. I'd controlled my diet — despite the pressures I faced, despite my loneliness, despite everything.

As winter set in and I had time off for Christmas, I explored different parts of Naples. I visited Vomero, which is just outside the city centre – a high end area where all the designer shops are situated.

As I walked along the stylish streets, I envied the glamorous women around me. They looked like models. They were tall and thin and dressed in designer gear. There I was, in purple tights and fishnet socks, wearing a vintage dress I'd bought from a flea market.

I wanted to look like them. If only I was as poised and elegant, I'd probably feel more confident in my own skin. Despite my paltry bank balance, I went shopping. I spotted an underwear shop that appeared more affordable and was pleased that they did knickers in my size – I'd lost that much weight that nothing fit me anymore. Luckily, in this part of the city, it was all size zeros and similar sizes. At that time, I was a small UK size 6, but I craved to be smaller. I felt that I wouldn't be truly happy until I was invisible.

The shop assistant wrapped my new underwear in sheets of tissue paper and placed it in a designer bag. I felt a wave of pride that I'd earned enough money to pay for them, and even better still, that I was a shadow of my former size (UK 12-14).

I shuddered as I left the shop and felt the cold weather pierce my skin. That was it, I needed a new coat. I was drawn to the colour black because of how elegant it looked on the Italian women. Also, I wouldn't stand out in any way.

I found the perfect leather jacket, whose label said: 'Made in Italy'. It didn't protect me from the cold much, but I loved how I could blend in anywhere with it on.

It was almost dusk and I decided to have a coffee in one of the fashionable bars, though I felt I lacked style with what I'd chosen to put on that day. My flatmate had joined me by this point. Everyone else looked beautifully elegant yet casual. They sipped aperitifs and enjoyed the free nibbles most bars laid out. Others drank Campari and lemonade and placed bread and pizza in their mouths.

I watched a stunning woman pick up a slice of freshly made pizza. She folded it over and took a bite. Mozzarella and salami seeped over the edge of the carb-laden snack. How can she eat that without thinking? How can she laugh whilst consuming all those calories? Why was I so obsessed by pizza? It wasn't as if I craved it; in fact, I feared it.

Carbs, by this point, had started to feel like threatening weapons that could attack me at any moment, and I was surrounded.

I wondered if the woman would make her excuses and rush to the toilet to rid herself of the poison she'd just eaten. She didn't. She remained with her friends, content and beautiful.

I realised that the black coffee I was drinking had sugar in it. I started to panic. I rushed to the loo, clumsily bumping into people; it felt like they were clawing me as I passed. I'd become so frail that every knock felt like a punch.

Once I'd made myself sick, I looked at myself in the full-length mirror. My face looked swollen, my hands were bloody, and my make-up was smeared. I quickly smoothed over the stripes in my blusher where tears had trickled down my cheeks. I swilled my mouth with water and put on some lip-gloss. I'd become used to this routine, I just hated doing it in public. At least the amount I consumed was easier to control in a bar — I couldn't binge.

I felt exhausted, but I hadn't had a night out in ages, and we were in one of the nicest areas of the city. I was determined that caffeine and music would see me through the night.

As I made my way back to our table, I spotted an attractive man. He had sandy blonde hair and sun-kissed skin. He wore a crisp blue shirt that was tucked into his designer jeans; the colour highlighted his eyes.

I sighed. He was too good for me. I looked down at the floor as I pushed through the throng of people.

I jumped as a palm pressed into the delicate skin of my back. It was him.

I felt myself turning bright red. The bar's lighting was dim, thankfully. The man spoke in Italian and introduced himself as Alexandro. His voice was silky-smooth, and I understood him well enough. I explained that I was English and living in Italy for a year.

Close-up, I definitely thought he was too good for me. He kept asking me questions, trying to strike up a conversation. I didn't have the confidence to speak to someone so beautiful.

Surely, he couldn't fancy me. Had he seen my swollen cheeks? Had he not spotted my red knuckles and big hips? I'd been out all day — I wasn't even dressed for a night out.

But he kept chatting to me. Then his friend came over, who was equally as handsome, but with dark hair and skin. I ushered them both over to the table where my flatmate waited. They joined us for a drink, and I even allowed myself to have alcohol; I needed some Dutch courage to chat to this man.

We then went to another bar, and another. He knew everyone…some of the most beautiful women I've ever seen waved at him.

By this time, he was clutching my hand. He'd even put his jacket over my shoulders as I was shivering. Why wasn't he embarrassed to be seen with someone as ugly and broken as me?

He didn't seem deterred. We ended up dancing and kissing in an underground bar. I'd only had a few drinks, but I felt tipsy as I hadn't touched alcohol for months. It actually felt good to let my hair down.

We danced until the bar closed then we piled into a cafe. In England, a typical student night out meant binge drinking followed by a kebab. In Italy, it was a couple of drinks with food, some dancing, then on to an espresso bar to drink coffee and eat croissants at the end of the night.

I didn't mind an espresso, but when everyone began to bite into croissants and pastries, I started to worry about how I could avoid joining in. I explained I wasn't hungry, even though I was famished — I'd drunk alcohol, been dancing all night and shopping all day. Even if I'd been told that I would die otherwise, nothing would have made me eat the block of butter encased in dough, sprinkled with sugar – which is how my mind saw croissants.

My friend and the two men chatted whilst eating and drinking. I ordered some sparkling water and another espresso. Hopefully, I'd have enough energy to get home.

Eventually, we said goodbye to the guys, and my friend and I took a taxi back to our apartment. By this point I was absolutely ravenous. My blood sugar had dropped, and I couldn't think straight. I still had some flavourless vegetable soup in the fridge. The water from the soup would fill me up enough that I wouldn't feel tempted by my flatmate's food.

I sat with my soup at the small dining table in the poky kitchen. My flatmate leant against the kitchen counter as she lathered butter onto a crusty French loaf. She always snacked on bread when she was hungry.

Bread was a staple of my childhood, particularly at my dad's house. With every meal, slices of thick, white bread would be stacked in the centre of the table. Between the four of us, we could easily polish off almost an entire loaf, making sandwiches out of whatever was on our plates – from Sunday roasts to instant noodles. In Italy, it was the same. Bread was always crusty and freshly made at the local bakery. People would have drawers full of bread to eat with meals – as a snack, and as a breakfast with jams and plenty of butter.

Now, bread was my enemy. I was tortured by the thought of how full it would make me. I feared I would be like the kid in Charlie and the Chocolate Factory, swelling up like a balloon if so much as a crumb entered my mouth.

I eventually went to bed. I felt happy because I'd met Alexandro and his friend – I still couldn't believe someone so good-looking was interested in me. It must be my English accent, I thought.

I convinced myself that I needed a new wardrobe, and that I needed to lose some fat from my face, so that it wouldn't be obvious that I was 'punching above my weight', so to speak.

By the time I woke Alexandro had already sent a text. He

wondered if my friend and I wanted to meet them again. He suggested meeting at a gelateria. I tried not to focus on this and figured that everywhere served coffee; I could avoid the ice-cream.

Sadly, the date was dull. We just drove around a few sights in the city. Even between four of us there was nothing to talk about. I could barely think of what to say in Italian to make conversation. Still, I wanted him to like me, to fancy me, to give me some sort of redemption. I could put up with someone boring and vain if I knew they liked me.

*

The cold continued its attack. I shuddered with every gust of wind; I layered long socks over tights and wore two coats, but I could not get warm.

I'd made friends with a lot of families — one of them ran the local chocolaterie. I'd stand inside the sweet-smelling shop as chocolates were being made — the smell alone gave me a high. By this point, I'd stopped craving sweet things and I would simply gaze at the handcrafted chocolates, seeing them as little pellets of poison.

When I met with friends for breakfast I'd stick to espressos whilst they devoured sweet delicacies, from a Neapolitan Baba (a traditional dessert dipped in rum) to Cannoli Siciliana (a sweet pastry filled with ricotta, a white, rich cream). Watching them eat was like watching a cookery show on telly. I deconstructed their meals in my head and focused on the ingredients that went into each dish.

I wondered how they could eat, talk and drink without any fear of what might happen to them after consuming such things.

I even researched their favourite desserts. I discovered that Cannoli Siciliana, according to legend, was a decadent dessert with a 'sexy' history. As I learnt the reason why the sweet pastry was phallically-shaped, I thought about my depleting sex drive.

I had no desire to be intimate with anyone. My bones hurt if people even hugged me too hard. I was so focused on losing weight and being able to see my bones that I didn't have any desire for a man to touch me — though I did want men to love me and look after me.

The irony was that all the Italian men I'd befriended told me that they preferred curvier girls, and not someone with a boyish figure like the one I'd acquired. I didn't care. I felt proud that I could see my skeleton. I felt in control. I felt like I'd actually achieved something.

The more visitors I had from the UK, the more hassle I received about my weight, and the more I was forced to eat out. I felt angry and annoyed when people tried to encourage me to eat. It made no difference, really; I just made myself sick more often to get rid of anything I consumed during social gatherings. I hated it when people tried to get in the way of my goals, and also that I didn't have the strength to concentrate or the stamina to exercise. I mustered up the energy to walk everywhere, regardless; I needed to stay active.

As Christmas neared, I was invited to lots of events with the new friends I'd made. None of my clothes fit me anymore, so I decided to change my whole wardrobe. I felt so pleased that I could fit into the smallest sizes — and sometimes even children's clothes — in some of the boutiques I visited. I felt like a new person. My past nor the people around me could stop the Sophie I was becoming.

The time came for me to return home to the UK for Christmas. My family were shocked when they saw me, and they gave me an ultimatum. Either I returned home for good, voluntarily, or they'd endeavour to have me sectioned, due to my decreasing weight.

They said that my eating disorder was controlling me, but I maintained to myself that I was in control. I was managing so well and losing so much weight. The voice in my head — my 'friend' — was there to help me. My so-called loved ones were just trying to break us up.

Despite these thoughts I had a greater fear of being sectioned, so I agreed to stay in the UK. I couldn't bring myself to explain to my friends in Italy that I wouldn't be returning, as I was adamant that I would go back.

Back home, I jumped straight into my old life and started dancing again. I had to hold up my costumes; my skeletal body could barely hold the weight of the skirts.

I reasoned to myself that, because I could still wear the outfits — though only just — I needed to lose more weight. I didn't want to fit into anything from my past, even my recent past. In my eyes, there was still fat on my legs and face to lose. I would not stop until all I could see was bone.

I had a couple of big gigs that Christmas. I feared showing off the fat still left on my body, but I couldn't afford to turn the money down.

The first gig was in my home city of Sheffield. I was so nervous. I couldn't concentrate or remember any routines; when the time came I just had to wing it.

Looking in the dressing room mirror. I was pleased to see my concave stomach, my hip bones jutting out and my frail, stick-thin arms. But my face...it was still round and my cheeks were still chubby.

It was soon time to go on stage. Performing suddenly felt like the loneliest thing on Earth. My body ached as I took my starting position.

The spotlight shone in my eyes then adrenaline kicked in. Fortunately, my body went with the music — it had danced to the song so many times, it instinctively knew what to do.

I became aware that my body felt strange. It moved in a different way than before. My bones jarred with every beat and my once-fluid hip movements felt rigid and awkward. The event was a charity ball dinner. I could see some of the tables where people sat watching. One man caught my eye and he offered up his plate of food to me. The audience burst out laughing; it must have been obvious how much weight I'd lost.

I wanted to hide but I couldn't...the show had to go on.

I fulfilled all my bookings during the festive period and even found myself in Dublin with some top stars in an exclusive show. I didn't enjoy it. I could barely stand, let alone dance. It was only my stubbornness and sheer determination that saw me through.

I avoided going outdoors, where possible; the cold, by this point, stung my skin. My body felt like it would snap in the wind. I couldn't share my thoughts and feelings with my friends and family, as they were concerned enough about my weight.

Christmas Day came, with all its gluttony and indulgence. As a child, I used to live for Christmas Day. Chocolate and croissants for breakfast, washed down with orange juice and coffee, followed by more chocolates, Christmas dinner, then leftovers and even more chocolate.

Not that Christmas Day. I prayed that nobody would be so cruel as to buy me chocolate. And what was I going to do about Christmas dinner? How could I avoid it?

At breakfast I reluctantly sat around the table whilst my family enjoyed croissants. I kept thinking, 'There's a block of butter in each of those. I wonder if they'd make themselves sick if they knew.'

I clutched my cup of black coffee. We'd already had a drama that morning when Dad had spiked it with a dash of milk by accident. I was vegetarian, not vegan, but my reaction was more to do with unnecessary calories than anything else.

Thankfully, my family let me sip coffee and push my croissant around the plate. Next, it was time to give out presents. As per usual, I received a Terry's Chocolate Orange in my stocking. Instead of feeling repulsed, it actually gave me a warm feeling; it reminded me of Christmases past. I dared myself to take a slice to prolong the feeling of nostalgia.

As everyone opened the rest of their presents, I kept telling myself over and over: 'Come on, Sophie, just enjoy it. It's Christmas.'

My dad headed to the kitchen to start Christmas dinner. I sat in my PJs, looking at my gifts. I couldn't stop fantasising about the chocolate orange.

I took a bite of another slice. The sweet creamy texture gave me an instant kick. It tasted so good. I felt a rush of energy pass through me.

My 'friend' inside me said, 'You've just eaten bad food. You don't deserve it. You must rid yourself of the poison.'

I left my sister watching TV and said I was going to the bathroom. I turned on the shower to make some noise whilst I hovered over the toilet. Would this be what I associated with Christmas from now on? Bent double, with my sharp nails down my throat, I tried to rid my stomach of the chocolate orange I'd eaten.

My body wouldn't purge. I tried harder to make myself vomit. The blood vessels in my face felt like they were going to explode. Eventually, I managed to bring up some of the chocolate and dregs of the coffee I'd had for breakfast. I took a shower and got dressed.

We'd invited some family friends over for Christmas dinner. The pressure of the day, sitting at the table, with everyone expecting me to eat, was just too much. After swirling soup around my bowl then nibbling on some vegetables, I made my excuses and went up to my bedroom.

The house was full of people, yet I felt so lonely. It was just me and the bully inside me. I lay under the covers and wished for the day to be over.

CHAPTER NINE

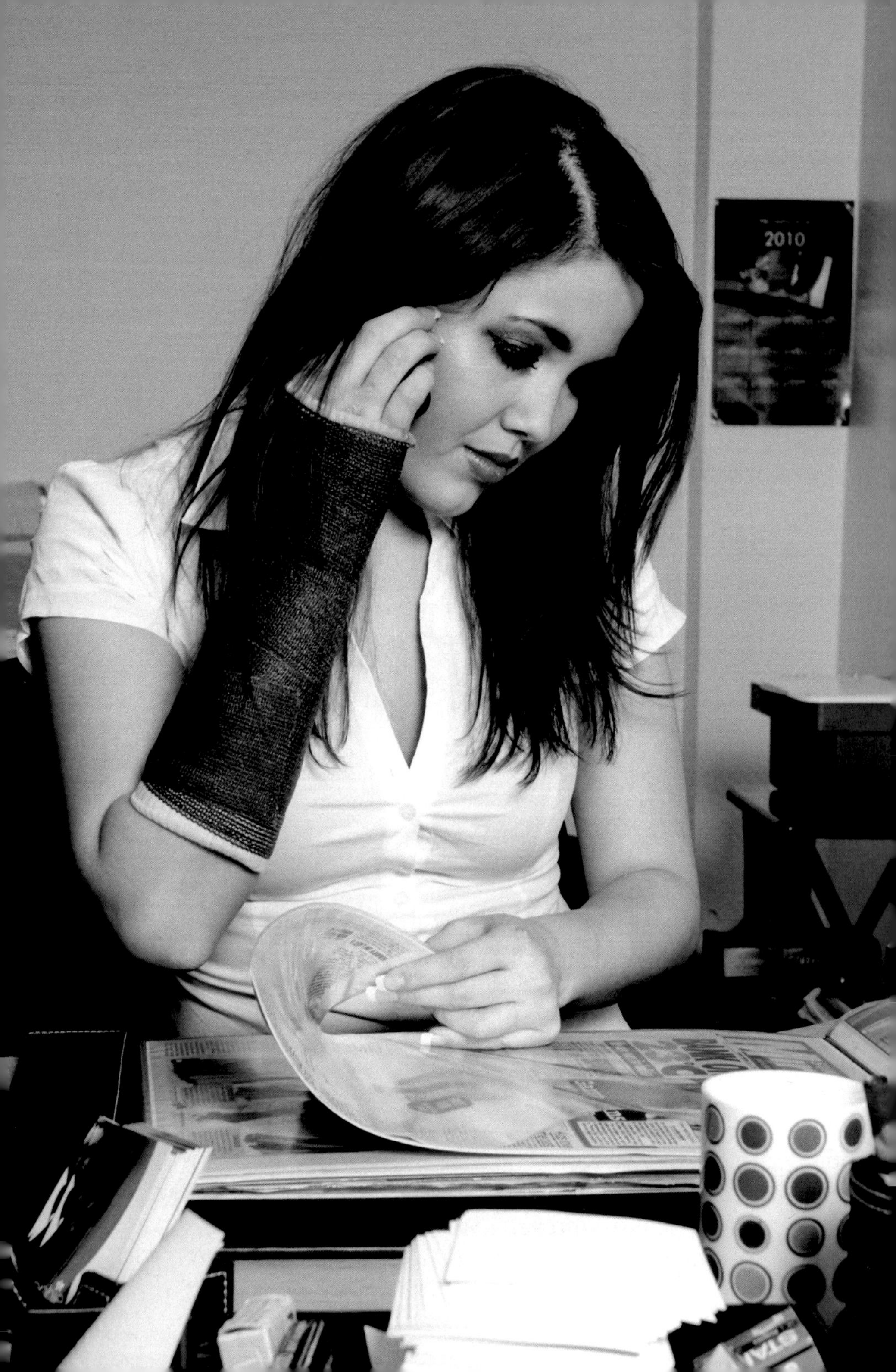
2010

'You haven't come this far, just to come this far.'
~ adaptation of Tom Brady's inspirational quote

Within weeks of returning to the UK, my bulimia well and truly made itself at home as I holed up in the attic bedroom of my mum's house.

My weight had crept up a little, which people saw as a good thing; what they didn't know was that the bully inside was gaining strength, not me.

I made the tough decision to defer from university, which hurt a lot. I felt a failure — all my friends were still on their year abroad and I'd had to return home.

My anxiety worsened once I came back. I doubt I'd have had the energy to return to Naples, even if I'd been allowed to. What hurt most was that I'd not given up on anything before that point. I would rather have killed myself than fail to finish something I'd committed to. It physically hurt to admit defeat, but I had no choice.

I'd lost all control. The outside world became a distant memory. I spent my time inside the attic, which became a makeshift torture chamber.

Anyone on the outside could have been forgiven for thinking I was getting better. Within a couple of months of returning home — to rest, recover and get better — I secured a job as a PR account manager, and I also set up my own dance school. And I still performed in shows. Work became my addiction.

During the day I'd be busy helping huge corporations with their PR and marketing, alongside running my own businesses. I thought work was a positive distraction from food and my bulimia, and I also had an innate drive to do 'big things'.

It was all just a distraction from the pain I felt inside. I was on autopilot; I got up at the crack of dawn to work on my own businesses, before walking to the PR agency (I could have caught a bus...but any excuse for more exercise). I worked all day, fuelled only by coffee and segments of fruit. Breaks and trips to the toilet were spent on my phone, returning emails and chasing business opportunities. After work, I either taught dance or I performed. When I eventually returned home at the end of the day, I'd dispose of any dinner my mum left me. I wouldn't sit with the family and eat their poisonous food; I'd instead go to the attic and hibernate.

At my computer I continued to work on my businesses until late at night, snacking on nuts and dates, and swigging as much sparkling water as possible. I took breaks to make myself sick, so I could then start all over again.

My work addiction fuelled my eating disorder, and vice versa. I excelled in both.

It felt like a double life. One of a highly successful, young career woman (who told people she'd left university to focus on her career), and the other of a child swamped by a cruel eating disorder that made her harm herself more than any other person could ever do.

As with anything I did, it was all or nothing. The more weight I put on, the more my eating disorder tightened its grasp. I did everything to try and keep my weight down; there was nothing more insulting to me than people saying, 'You're looking healthier. You look much better now you've gained some weight.' Each comment was like a knife twisting in my gut.

I couldn't have felt unhealthier. I was taking packets and packets of laxatives every night, buying diet pills and downing them by the tub. My knuckles were red raw. My throat continuously bled. My stomach was always bloated, and every time food passed through it, I was in pain.

I was either desperate for the toilet, due to the laxatives, or I'd be bent double with pain, because I couldn't go to the toilet.

The people around me began to pick up on my behaviour. My frequent trips to the toilet and the time I spent in there — purging, following a binge, or passing loose stools.

My whole life seemed to revolve around the attic and the toilet. Somehow, during the day, I managed to mask my behaviour. Only occasionally would my two worlds collide; usually, when I had to work late (which would, pardon the pun, eat into my bingeing and purging time). On these occasions, I'd cave in and end up grabbing something from the vending machine after a day spent starving myself. I'd then try and discreetly throw up in the staff toilets.

I felt disgusted and so ashamed of myself.

Worst still, my face, which I loathed so much, became even fatter and even puffier, thanks to constant purging. I imagined they looked like a hamster's cheeks and I dreamt of having my face reconstructed.

I plastered make-up on each day, to hide the blood vessels that had popped and to smooth over the puffiness. I wore huge fake eyelashes. I researched hair extensions, plastic surgery and permanent make-up — anything to cover up the mess I'd become. I was deeply unhappy. I'd look in the mirror and despise the clown I'd become.

I had a good job, a loving family, great friends, a successful dance career and my own enterprises. And yet I was the unhappiest and unhealthiest I'd ever been.

I felt so angry. Why couldn't my family have left me in Italy? I was in control there. People thought I'd recovered, but instead, I was deteriorating more than they knew.

I'd lost control of my life, my weight, my bowels…I'd lost control of myself. I felt empty…a machine. I tried to be as successful as possible at work, but behind closed doors, I was a mess.

By now, I was about to turn twenty-one, and I was determined to mark the milestone. I decided to hold a star-studded premiere for a documentary I'd made for ITV, about belly-dancing in Egypt. Once I set my sights on this event, that was it. It would be huge, with everyone I knew involved — the party of the century.

I had the work I dreamed of. I still had my smile, my drive and my passion. I was addicted to my career just as much as I was addicted to my relationship with the bully inside me. I would rather have died than give either obsession up.

I'd been on an NHS waiting list for treatment relating to my eating disorder, but as my weight was just within the normal range (even at my most skeletal, on returning from Italy), I wasn't a priority.

Each time I was rejected by the experts, I felt I'd failed. One day, four months after returning home from Italy, I'd had enough.

It had been an ordinary day at work, but a minor criticism from a client during a phone call tipped me over the edge.

I couldn't cope anymore. I couldn't deal with the criticism, yet no one hated me more than I hated myself. I hated myself for upsetting my family. I hated myself for leaving university. I hated myself for the way I looked. I hated the fact I spent all my hard-earned money on items that plastered over my insecurities.

I sat in my cesspit of a bedroom and drank neat vodka. I took as many of my tablets as I physically could before staggering out of the house. I'd already overdosed a number of times on laxatives, but this time I'd downed a cocktail of paracetamol, ibuprofen, antidepressants, laxatives and diet pills.

*

I woke up in hospital, confused. What had happened? Why was I there?

My family was stood around my bed. I felt a huge wave of guilt at what I'd put them through, but I was also disappointed that my suicide attempt had failed.

I don't know if I'd actually wanted to die, but anything was better than what my life had become.

I was discharged a short while later, with little in the name of treatment or follow-up appointments—just a visit from my mental health nurse, who himself seemed to have issues and rarely turned up for appointments.

Once again, I felt worthless. Despite almost dying, I still wasn't worthy of care. The only thing that truly cared about me was the bully inside.

CHAPTER
TEN

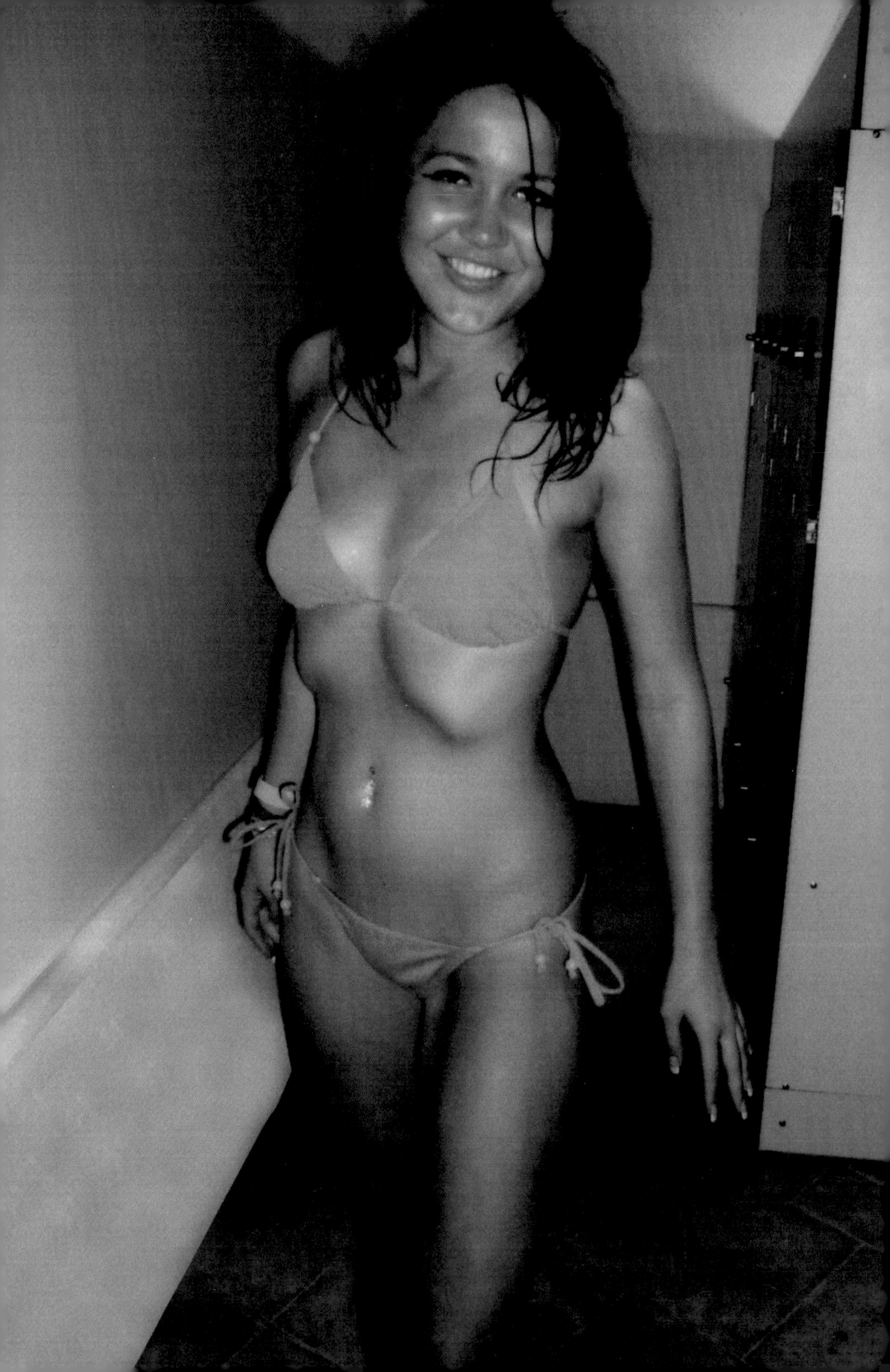

'Grant me the serenity to accept the things I cannot change, the courage to change the things I can, and wisdom to know the difference. Living one day at a time, enjoying one moment at a time. Accepting hardships as the pathway to peace.'

~ adaptation of The Serenity Prayer, Reinhold Niebuhr

Eventually, I reached the top of the waiting list and was offered an appointment. I'd left my job in PR—I explained my departure by saying I wanted to focus on my businesses; there was no way I wanted to admit that I'd had an overdose or that my health was struggling.

That wasn't a total lie, as I used the extra time I had to find a plush office for my own PR and marketing firm. I convinced myself that this was my next career move. I couldn't justify taking time out to recover or heal.

I wanted to be rid of my bulimic behaviours, but I couldn't let go of my bully. She may have driven me to insanity, but she also gave me the drive to succeed in my career. She gave me comfort, she gave me an outlet, and she stood by me.

I continued to live a double life. I regularly appeared in the press, due to my business and dance successes.

Would my dark secret come out one day? I worried about most aspects of my life; this was yet another thing to agonise over.

If ever things get too much, I'll end my life. And, next time, I'll do a proper job of it.

I attended an assessment at the Eating Disorder Centre. I was desperate for help, but I felt like I'd failed yet again, being curvier than I'd ever been. Would I be laughed out of the building? Would they reject me, like most GPs did?

This was my last chance. I knew my 'friend' inside was killing me. I only had a tiny bit of fight left.

I hadn't achieved all my career goals, so I focused on that. I couldn't justify getting better simply for my health and peace of mind, but I could for my career.

Nervously, I sat in a small room with a woman called Wendy. I studied her lean figure, her calm nature and her friendly smile.

She explained that they had to record my weight and height for their files. 'This is the worst part,' she said, 'and we can do it first. Get it out of the way.'

I cringed. I knew I was heavier than ever. I was so ashamed.

Wendy measured my BMI without flinching or passing comment. As the appointment continued, I was heartened that she saw past my weight, my height and my face. She genuinely seemed to want to help me.

After a couple of months of treatment with Wendy, it was clear that my eating disorder hadn't improved. She knew I needed more intensive help, but she was restricted to what she could offer, as it was underpinned by the patient's BMI. Despite what the scales said, Wendy was yet another professional who told me that my eating disorder was one of the worst she'd ever seen.

My weight may have been 'normal,' but my mind and physical health were definitely not. My potassium levels were tested regularly…this is a danger with bulimia. If your potassium is too low, you can die.

Wendy wrote a persuasive and compelling referral letter to the Eating Disorder Unit in Leeds, which is where I was sent. I was placed in a room on the 19-bed ward. I was surrounded by anorexics and I've never felt more of a failure than I did then.

Whilst it deeply shocked and saddened me to hear the woman in the next bed wail for help, I also envied her. She was a 'successful' anorexic, whereas I'd failed in that arena; I was a full-blown bulimic.

She was screaming and yelling, 'No! Stop!' It sounded like she was being violently attacked, but she was actually being fed a protein shake. It wasn't part of some weird diet, either. The young woman was so consumed with, and controlled by, her eating disorder she could no longer eat or drink without it being forced down her. I'm quite sure that, in those moments, she'd have preferred to be burnt at the stake.

I was trapped in the hospital unit with several other patients — all of whom were severely underweight. I was, in comparison, a 'healthy weight'. Yet I was beside my fellow inmates at death's door, even if I didn't look like it.

The bully inside me was inspired by the other patients' skeletal bodies. I desperately wanted to be like them and vowed to lose every ounce of fat and muscle from my body.

The one benefit of being a healthy weight was being allowed in the garden for some fresh air. Neither did I need a wheelchair to get there. When I did venture outside, I'd feel scared, because it meant mixing with patients from the psychiatric unit downstairs — the really mad ones, I thought. Still, it was better to be outside than in that stuffy unit.

Our bedroom windows barely opened, to prevent us from escaping or vomiting out of the window. There was a small pane of glass in the door to our rooms, however, so that they could observe us all day and all night.

I was allowed to use the shared toilet and shower without supervision — a luxury not everyone had. I broke the rules, however, and abused this trust by trying to make myself sick in the loo. As fizzy drinks were banned on the ward, vomiting was difficult to achieve.

My night-time incontinence returned. I was so embarrassed that, at twenty-one years old, I'd started to wet the bed again. It was so humiliating, and I tried to hide it from the nurses by sleeping on a sheet of plastic.

One morning a nurse came into my room to see how I was. I tried to pluck up the courage to explain that I needed new sheets, then she said, 'I hope you don't mind me asking...but were you on TV?'

I was mortified that she'd recognised me. That she knew just how much my reality TV 'fame' had come crashing down — to a point where I was stuck in a secure unit and sat on urine-soaked sheets.

We talked about Britain's Got Talent, and I cringed when I thought of where I was and what my life had become. Spending my days worrying about, and avoiding, food, until late at night, when I binged and purged for a release, then being trapped on a ward where food and mealtimes were everything. I had to convince myself that it would all be worth it — not just for my health, but so I could share my story one day.

In the unit, we had to get up for breakfast; mealtimes and snacks were compulsory. I had to obtain a letter confirming I was a lifelong vegetarian — no dietary preferences were allowed otherwise.

We had to eat in a small dining room where we were closely watched by staff. I hated being forced to eat everything they put in front of me. We weren't even allowed condiments to mask any flavours. And they lathered our toast with butter.

I hated it. I'd spend more than an hour looking at my food and picking at little bits...just enough to ensure I wasn't constantly pestered. I watched my fellow inpatients struggle. I was still determined to eat less than them, because I wanted to be skeletal, too. Being in the unit was a great way to lose weight, because I could starve myself. I didn't have access to food, so I couldn't binge.

I began to feel more in control and enjoyed that there was less chaos in my life, though I hated the routine. In our free time, i.e. when we weren't having blood tests, therapy or a meal, we could relax in our rooms or sit in the communal lounge.

I was too embarrassed to go into the lounge, as so many women knew each other well — they'd been in and out of the unit for years. I also couldn't relax enough to watch daytime TV or flick through the magazines laid out for us (any diet features or triggering pictures were removed prior, so as not to encourage patients).

Instead, I retreated to my room where I had my laptop. I'd brought boxes of my accounts from home; I thought being in hospital would be a good opportunity to get my boring admin tasks done — with no distractions, other than dreaded mealtimes.

One lunchtime, whilst staring at my jacket potato that was soaked in butter and covered in baked beans and cheese, a new female patient came in. She was friendly and a newbie like me; she wasn't a 'lifer' like a lot of the others — this was a new experience for her, too. She may also have been deemed 'successful' by society — she worked as a university lecturer, specialising in Media and Body Image.

We had a lot in common. I knew what it felt like to promote a 'positive body image' through belly-dancing whilst also struggling myself. I found it hard being a strong leader in a field where I also felt vulnerable.

Whilst in the unit, I quickly began to lose weight and my bloods got worse, as I refused to eat the food they gave me. I'd reluctantly dip a spoon in sloppy Weetabix for breakfast and lick it clean, but it really was an ongoing internal battle. The 'people pleaser' part of me wanted to do as I was told, but my internal raging bully was convinced that the doctors and nurses were out to poison me. I had to choose: my bully or the professionals. I chose my friend, the bully.

Due to my non-compliance of the diet set for me, and the fact I was a 'normal' weight (even though I actually lost weight in the centre), I was sent home for 48 hours, to reflect on whether I would stay in the hospital and adhere to their rules.

Yet again, I felt like a failure. Rejected. So, whilst I had the chance, I discharged myself permanently. I couldn't face the embarrassment or pain of going back there.

I didn't want to recover. I didn't want to get rid of the bully inside me. She was all I had.

I returned home and the cycle continued. I went straight back to work, back to appointments with Wendy, and back to my old habits of bingeing and purging — memories of the hellish unit at the forefront of my mind.

I had to be careful. I couldn't allow myself to be sectioned, which was the next step.

CHAPTER ELEVEN

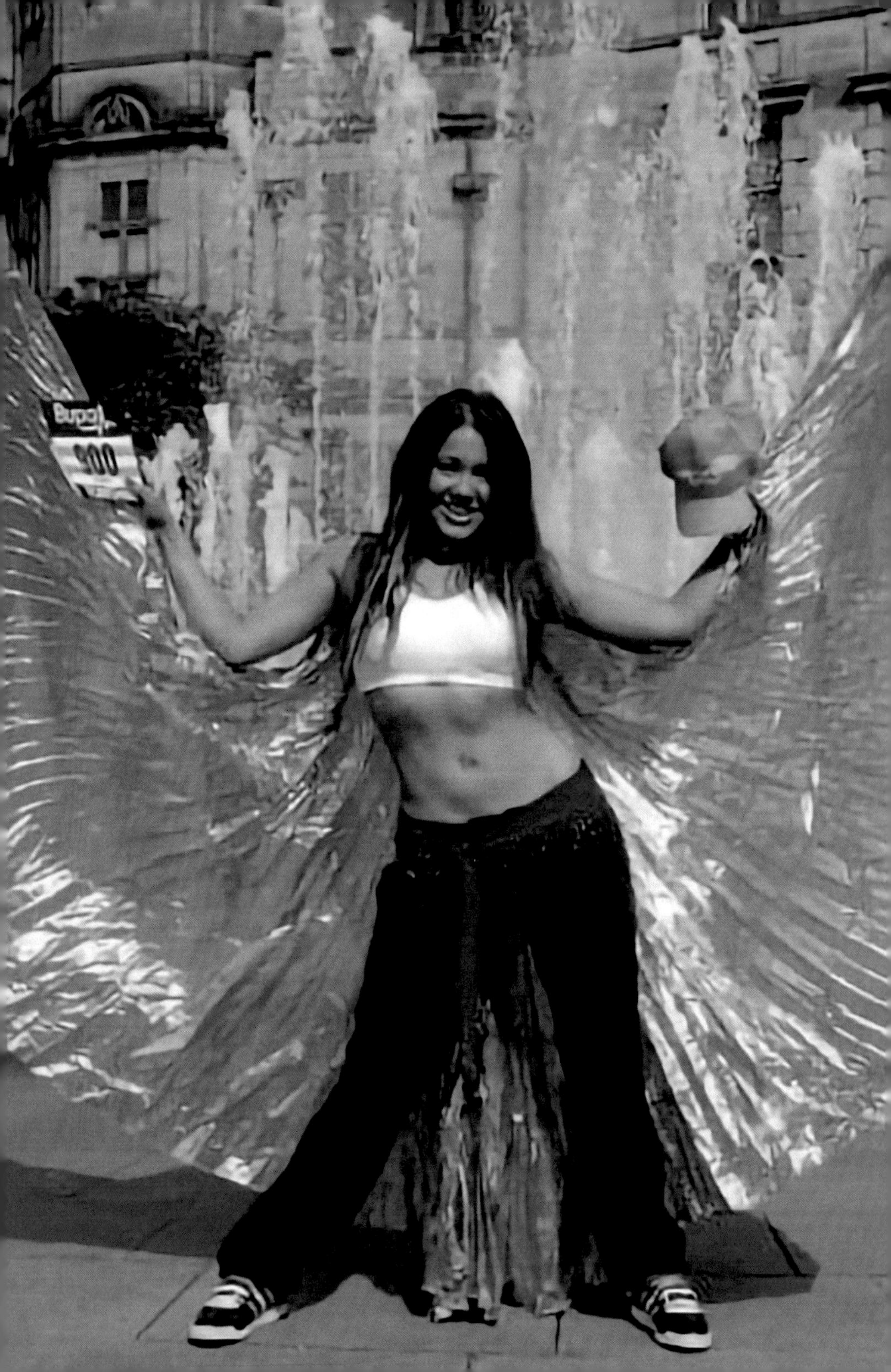

*'Imperfection is beauty, madness is genius and it's better to be absolutely
ridiculous than absolutely boring.'*
~ Marilyn Monroe

By this point, I felt rejected in every way. Rejected by the health
services, rejected by society…rejected by my own body.

I continued to work hard. I even skipped health appointments,
because work was my priority, not my health. I began drinking
alcohol again when attending evening events, as a way to escape
and feel more confident. I looked like a party girl to others, yet I
wanted to hide.

I fell back on my old habit of seeking male attention. I thought it
would make me feel better about myself.

I was younger than most people at the business events I attended,
which meant I stood out. I hated networking and 'schmoozing' but I
knew it was important if I wanted to grow my business.

One day, I got chatting to a charismatic businessman. He was
charming, confident, he ran lots of businesses, and he was almost
double my age. I loved the thought that he might look after me…
maybe even protect me.

We started dating. He took me to all his favourite bars and
restaurants, wining and dining me. I tried to avoid the food and just
focused on getting drunk.

He even offered to take me away for the weekend. I tried to
get out of it; as much as I loved the idea, I was addicted to using
laxatives and was still wetting the bed.

He wouldn't take no for an answer. He'd already booked us a
series of trips around the UK for 'romantic breaks'. It was on these
trips that our age gap became apparent. He'd want to listen to
sixties' music, watch tribute bands and eat stodgy food. I wanted to
dance to pop music, explore places or simply relax.

He bought us bottle after bottle of wine and constantly topped my
glass up. He seemed the perfect gentlemen until the alcohol kicked
in.

Once I was drunk, he'd berate me for drinking, even though he'd
encouraged it. I then 'owed him' when it came to the bedroom and

sexual activity.

I did what I could to please him but his rules constantly changed, so that I was always indebted to him. I thought he cared about me, because he'd treated me to the trip, even though I hadn't wanted to go. He paid for everything and he made sure I knew that. I constantly offered to pay, but he wouldn't let me.

At night, after we'd had sex and he finally fell asleep, I lay awake, trying not to wet the bed. I was so scared about having an accident that I went to the toilet constantly through the night.

By now, I'd moved into my own one-bedroom flat. This guy called me in-between every business meeting. I could never sit down and do my work. I also wasn't allowed to walk round when I spoke to him; he insisted that I did nothing other than sit and talk to him.

Our next trip was to London, where we stayed in a plush boutique hotel. We went shopping in all the designer stores in Kensington, and I felt like I was in the Pretty Woman film. My man-friend either bought me things he wanted me to wear or he'd encourage me to spend my money on items I could barely afford.

But this was still living the dream, wasn't it?

After an expensive meal (he always chose the restaurant, which I didn't mind, as most of them had few vegetarian options and this meant I could avoid eating), we went to a high-end bar. Everyone there looked so stylish and I felt like a common frump.

He kept buying bottles of the most ridiculously priced champagne. Eventually, I could barely stand. I realised I hadn't seen him for a while, but just assumed he'd gone to the bar.

Then I saw his big grin and his piercing eyes staring…not at me, but at another woman he was chatting to. I was actually grateful for a break from him and I started texting my friends.

I felt a tug at my shoulder. He was back, with the woman in tow. He introduced me as his girlfriend, and I could see the shock on the woman's face; she'd clearly not realised we were together.

I smiled at her sheepishly. As the woman tried to make her excuses, he put his arm around her, and said, 'Don't worry. I wanted to introduce you both as I thought we could all have some fun together.'

My heart sank. I wasn't going to get any respite from him; instead, he was angling for a threesome. Fortunately, the woman removed his hand and walked off. He didn't even flinch, just muttered, 'Her loss, fucking slag.'

As the relationship continued so did his grip on me. What had once been things he'd found attractive about me, he now hated. He absolutely loathed me dancing.

I had a huge gig coming up in London's Hyde Park. I tried to hide it from him, but when he found out I was dancing, I got a series of angry phone calls and messages. I'd disobeyed him. I would be punished.

The wave of adrenaline that washes over me whenever I perform gave me a sense of confidence. As he ranted away on the phone, I told him we were over.

That night, when I returned home, he continued to send messages. They became more and more aggressive, then he said he was coming over to my flat.

I knew he'd act out his threats, so I jumped over my balcony and ran to the local shop. I stayed in there for ages; I knew he wouldn't hurt me in public — he was all about putting on a good act.

Eventually, a friend came and picked me up and I stayed at her place.

I had a lucky escape. I felt guilty for ending it that way after he'd treated me so much, but I couldn't bear the thought of sleeping with him again or doing any of the things he wanted me to do to him. It made me feel physically sick.

*

There was a gym near my flat and I began training there. I'd get up, do some work, go to the gym, work in the gym's café, train some more, then work some more.

I'd finally found something positive to help me cope with my work and food addictions. Exercise didn't stop me from working hard or making myself sick, but it slowed down how often I'd overwork, binge and purge each day. Anything was better than nothing.

I decided to complete my university studies — but distantly, so

I didn't have to move back to Manchester, which had proved a huge trigger. I didn't have the confidence or capacity to make new friends; I just wanted to do the minimum necessary to get the degree I'd set out to achieve.

I was really interested in social issues and injustices, and mental health, but I didn't feel that, with my chosen subjects — philosophy and Italian — I could explore these things. If I'm honest, I struggled with philosophy; it was quite mathematical, nothing like the debate sessions we'd had at school on human rights issues. I also avoided going to Italian classes, as they reminded me of what I'd left in Naples.

When I did go into uni, I focused on one project: an online human rights magazine. This was a great outlet for me as I'd always wanted to be a broadcast journalist. It meant I could research stories I was passionate about yet still complete a community award with my university.

I was lucky that I had a vast network of people — from the charities I volunteered for, to the shisha bars I belly-danced at; I discovered a plethora of suitable stories.

I used the contacts I'd made when interviewed about my belly-dancing and applied for work experience at the BBC in Sheffield and Manchester, as well as at various local newspapers. Journalism felt like my calling.

I had my own story and difficult past, which helped me to understand others and speak out against injustice.

I threw myself into my work experience like I did every other passion. I was full of ideas, ambition and optimism.

I finally felt as if my life was moving forward. I received a lot of comments about my work experience — people thought I'd 'made it' because I'd done TV, and, at times, I felt embarrassed. Others wouldn't take me seriously; I was labelled as 'one of those people from reality telly'. I also received negativity from within the media industry for continuing to perform as a belly-dancer, even though it helped pay for my travel whilst I gained experience.

Despite feeling like an outsider, my stubbornness came to my rescue. I'd found a career I was good at, and yet another where it paid not to fit in. No other journalist I met had the network or contacts I had. A lot of them had been helped by their parents and influential family friends to get where they were. I found that my community database was far more important, in terms of stories — though maybe not as useful for promotions or paid work.

I skipped a number of lectures to meet up with case studies for my magazine and to find ideas for campaigns I could run that would help seldom heard communities. Without realising it, I discovered several 'scoops'. A few of my stories even went viral.

Whilst I struggled to secure paid work in journalism — as I didn't have the right contacts for that or the qualifications — my own work did really well. I was pleased, but I still wasn't confident of my abilities. Everything I did, I thought I could always do better.

I received funding for the online magazine, so that it would continue to help a wide range of communities to share their stories. I made the decision to not waste time any more time travelling to Manchester for lectures. Instead, I would continue to run my own businesses, further my journalism dream, and complete my studies from home. As my passion drove me to succeed, my eating disorder reared its head again, and it was much worse when I worked from home on my own. Not even writing or going to the gym stopped it, it just delayed some habits.

My mum suggested I moved back in with them, where I could have an office and bedroom. I was scared to be around other people, in case they picked up on my habits around work, eating and purging. On the other hand, I felt it would be nice to have the security of not paying rent and more time to focus on my work, gym and studies.

The only thing that got me out of the house and away from my laptop screen was exercise, either a trip to the gym or my new-found hobby of running. Even when I could barely open my eyes on a morning, when my face was puffed up from purging, I'd still drag myself to a gym class.

The gym brought me a new network of people who were predominantly positive influences. I also got a job there on weekends, teaching dance. So much of my focus was on the gym and journalism that I began to loathe studying. I no longer believed in academia, it wasn't for people like me.

I tried to find work experience in London — I thought it would be a fresh start and I'd finally be 'living the dream'. I'd also begun dating a colleague at the gym, which gave me something else to focus on.

I truly thought my life was falling into place when I won an International Media Award for the magazine I'd started at university. I was presented the award at a star-studded ceremony in London that was full of journalists I admired and respected. I couldn't believe I'd achieved something so huge.

I made the most of the event and chatted to loads of editors. Having a different background to others starting out in the industry helped me this time. I managed to secure placements at The Sunday Times, Channel 4 News, ITV News and The Guardian.

The only drawback was that I had my end of year university exams to complete first. I did what I'd always done: I shut myself away and studied hard, using my habits as a crutch to see me through. It was different this time, in that I only wanted to do the minimum needed.

Once my exams were over, my work placements began. I couldn't afford to stay in London for long, so most placements lasted just a day or two, rather than the usual two weeks.

I went into the placements full of ideas for investigations about human rights issues in the UK that hadn't already been covered. I dreamt about making and presenting documentaries and giving a voice to people like me who didn't fit the norm.

Editors noticed my enthusiasm and offered me paid work. At the same time, I decided to qualify as a personal trainer and dance instructor. Nothing was going stop me now.

One day, whilst working on the desk of a national newspaper, I started to feel sick. It was a weird sensation to physically feel sick rather than the torture of making myself sick. I really didn't feel myself and, as I sat typing at my computer, I suddenly remembered the night I'd got drunk on a date. I'd drunk too many 'fish bowls' and the night ended with me throwing up.

Surely, I couldn't be pregnant? Due to my eating disorder, I'd been told that I may struggle to conceive.

I left the office when it was my lunch break, which was unlike me. Normally, I'd stay at my desk and work through lunch, but I had to buy a pregnancy test. I went to the Boots inside Kings Cross station and flinched at the price of pregnancy tests.

Was there really a chance I could be pregnant? I couldn't cope with not knowing and bought three different types of tests. I rushed back to the office and to the staff toilets. I couldn't tell anyone; I was still only on polite terms with most people as I was too nervous to make friends. And being a (potentially 'up the duff' by a guy she'd just met) 'commoner' from the North was not typical in that newsroom — everyone seemed much more high-brow than me.

I shut the heavy toilet door behind me and read through the instructions.

After peeing on the stick, I nervously waited, my eyes fixated on the line. To my horror, another faint line emerged.

It must be wrong! I can't be…

I tried all the other sticks and they said the same.

I spent the afternoon googling 'false positive pregnancy tests' and learnt that, apparently, you can see a false negative but not the opposite. I was pregnant. The father was my colleague from the gym. We'd only been dating a couple of months.

That night, as I tried to sleep on the floor of my friend's bedsit in London, my mind whirled. My friend was a fellow creative, she'd got me my job in Italy; she was the only one who knew about my predicament.

Another pregnancy test I bought said I was several weeks pregnant.

I knew I had to return home to Sheffield to work out what I was going to do. I was petrified, but I also had a feeling of relief that, despite damaging my body for years with my eating disorder, my body had managed to create a new life. It was actually functioning as it should.

CHAPTER
TWELVE

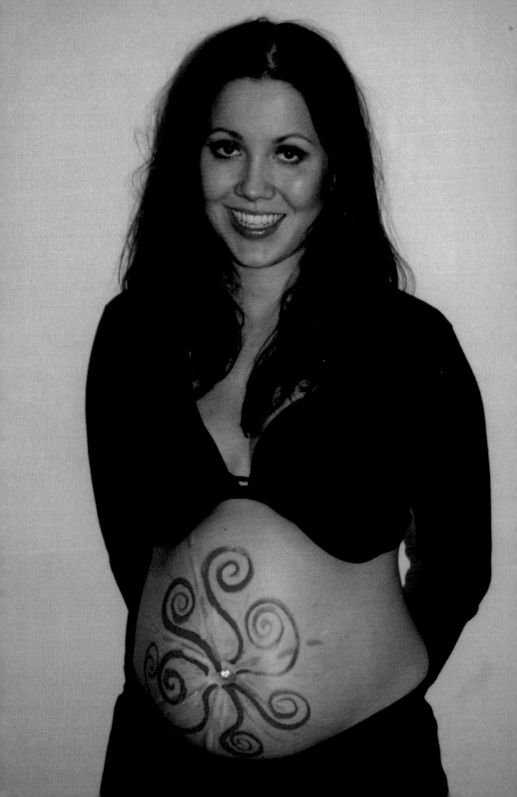

'If at first you don't succeed, dust yourself off and try again.'
~ Aahliyah

I somehow passed my university studies and was on the cusp of
a career high in London; now, at twenty-three, I was pregnant.
There was no way I could move south and juggle a baby and
career on my own — I'd have to freelance from Sheffield and
travel to London when needed.

Suffering from mental health problems and having an eating
disorder meant I was high risk when it came to antenatal care. I
thought this was brilliant; for once, despite my weight, I would
receive good, consistent support.

More people were involved in my life than ever before: eating
disorder services, a community mental health team, a Sure Start
centre referral, and extra appointments with a midwife and
health visitor. I was finally a priority. Bizarrely, I felt better than I
had for years. Pregnancy meant I'd given up alcohol and reduced
my sessions at the gym (though this gave me more time to do
work). An instinct to nurture my body and my baby also kicked
in.

It was incredible to witness the things my body could do
instinctively. This inner peace really helped when I felt waves
of bulimia coming (morning sickness stopped me from making
myself sick, though I still felt the urge to do so. I also longed to
cut myself). The physical and mental shifts really helped me.

I hadn't planned to have children until I was in my mid-
thirties. By then, I imagined my career would have taken off
and I'd have achieved some of my goals — such as making and
presenting documentaries.

I moved back to Yorkshire — to Wakefield — to be with my
baby's father, Richard, who lived with his parents.

I didn't dare tell the editors I worked for that I was pregnant. I
wanted them to give me freelance work, and I also felt I was at a
crucial point in my career.

I used the time I gained — away from the gym, commuting and
being apart from my friends and family in Sheffield — to focus on

working from home (well, Richard's parents' kitchen table).

At that time, I was working for a number of production companies as a researcher, and I was full of ideas and passion. It meant hours on the phone, hammering for case studies and researching different angles for various programmes.

I struggled with the monotony and loneliness of working remotely, though I enjoyed the flexibility. I could attend all my health appointments without having to explain to a boss that I was pregnant or had mental health problems. I could keep up the facade that I was a strong, young journalist who would do anything to bring a great story to air.

After pitching lots of story ideas and proposals, I finally had a few commissioned. Whilst producers used their own 'star' presenters, I was proud to be working on stories I was passionate about and shining a light on various communities.

I had to do most of the leg work and investigative side of things. I worked on two big stories for national news channels; I couldn't believe I was working alongside some of my idols.

I was too involved in these documentaries to turn round and say, 'I'm pregnant!', but luckily, I wasn't showing much (thanks to genetics and my belly-dancing) and I was able to conceal my bump. I wouldn't let pregnancy stand in my way of success.

I began to miss some health appointments as I became increasingly involved in my work. I was determined to get both pieces finished before I gave birth.

At times, investigating meant driving around, undercover, in hire cars and waiting around for dangerous criminals. I cared deeply about my unborn child and had stopped making myself sick, even though I was stressed, but I didn't care much for my own safety.

I still taught, and performed, belly-dancing—it provided a good, regular income, as opposed to the peaks and troughs of working in the media and invoicing editors once lengthy projects had finally completed.

Maybe I could 'have it all'. Maybe I could be a supermum who travelled the world, reporting on game-changing stories and uncovering human rights abuse with my baby in tow. It was a dream far removed from the nest I was making in Wakefield.

I consciously made an effort to break out of my isolation and media bubble and tried to get to know people in the area; I knew I'd need a support network when the baby came. I tried to attend as many groups and networks as my work schedule allowed. I offered my services as a journalist to write newsletters for charitable groups I became involved with, as well as belly-dancing sessions for new mums.

My diary became crammed with work and baby-related interests; I had no time to focus on my health and wellbeing. I wanted to do what was best for my work and my baby. I yearned to please my colleagues and impress my bosses, but I also wanted the best setting for my unborn child.

Granted, living in a room in my boyfriend's parents' house was not how I planned motherhood, but I made the best of the situation.

One morning, I got an urgent call from my editor. He said that one of my stories was being broadcast that night, and I needed to find, film and interview case studies that day. I panicked first and foremost, then adrenaline kicked in and I cancelled all my appointments. I was suffering from terrible morning sickness at that point, so I shoved plain baguettes and water into my bag to sustain myself as well as stave off any natural urge to retch.

I jumped on the train and travelled across Yorkshire to find some strong interviewees. As I whizzed around the county, my bump put pressure on my pelvis; I may have been waddling and panting, but this was my moment to shine.

I managed to track down some compelling case studies and got set to link up with one of the celebrity reporters. A last-minute call informed me that the reporter was stuck in traffic—I'd have to conduct the interview.

I was dressed in frumpy maternity gear, so I quickly rushed into a shop to buy something smarter. The panic and the stress became too much for me and I fainted.

I came round to find I was surrounded by people. I didn't

dare tell them I was pregnant as I didn't want them to call an ambulance. I had to get the story done. I got up, quickly bought a dress, and went and did the interview.

I worked right up until the birth. I wasn't going to allow myself time off. I was self-employed — not only would I not receive any maternity pay from an employer, I was also frightened to leave the rat race for fear of being forgotten or losing work. Despite my intentions, I didn't manage to finish one of the news documentaries before I had my daughter; I ended up being induced, which threw me off my work schedule earlier than expected.

I worried that I wouldn't be able to get a continuous phone signal in hospital — I didn't want any editor to think I'd gone off radar. I confided in a few colleagues on a need-to-know basis. They were really supportive and encouraged me to have time off, but I couldn't be sure that I'd return to the exact same point. There was always someone ready to work in the media and I saw myself as easily replaceable.

Whilst being induced was a nuisance, I liked that it gave me time to create some handover notes. I wasn't going to risk a story not going to air just because I was pushing out a baby. I was scared about giving birth, but I told myself that women had been doing it forever; I had to put up and shut up and keep on working.

The day I was to be induced, the hospital called to say that it wouldn't be until late afternoon or early evening. My dad took the family out for a big Chinese banquet to celebrate, before I went into hospital.

I told myself that it was the last treat. Once the baby was here, I'd be back on a diet. The meal was delicious — dim sum, my absolute favourite. We were in an underground restaurant that reminded me of meals out as a child when visiting family in Malaysia. The drawback was that they had poor phone signal; I felt a wave of panic that work colleagues or case studies may not be able to reach me.

The process of being induced was slow and traumatic.

Eventually, I was officially in labour. I began to feel worried — my life was going to change within hours. Would I be a good mother? Would I be able to breastfeed? I'd been so focused on my work that I hadn't prepared myself for the impending arrival.

My phone rang. It was a case study I'd been trying to get hold of for weeks. Should I grit my teeth through the pain and take it? Or should I ignore the call and suffer whatever consequences that brought? My editors wouldn't have expected me to take the call, but I wanted to impress them. These were the lengths I was prepared to go to, to get my work done.

I answered the phone and pretended I was at home. I managed to conduct a quick interview in-between contractions.

Hours later, my daughter Jasmine Mei India Hale was born. I wailed, out of fear and relief, that this mini-human was finally here, safe and sound. It was love at first sight. She settled in my arms, skin-to-skin, and started to feed from my breast.

I had to stay in hospital overnight, being high risk, though I refused to eat the food the hospital gave me. It was full of carbs, and I'd vowed that, once the baby came, I would no longer eat for two.

At home with my newborn, visitors arrived to meet her. They'd bring a variety of stodgy foods and sweet treats, so that I could 'keep up my energy levels'. I kindly refused and offered the chocolates, biscuits and cake to other guests.

When family came, they'd order from the local chippy and try to treat me, but I was tired, low, and all I heard was the bully inside me.

I found motherhood amazing and it really shows you what's really important in life. Nobody tells you the toll it takes on your mind and body. Overnight, you lose your identity. Your hormones are everywhere. You feel vulnerable and crave to be looked after, but you must forget your needs to care for an even more vulnerable creature.

I understood why my Chinese relatives followed the traditional '40 days indoors' rule after giving birth.

During this period of unpredictability — of not knowing when

I'd be able to sleep or eat; of my brain feeling like mush — I returned to old habits to gain some control and tightened up my rules around food.

I set myself a strict routine that consisted of baby groups, mother and baby exercise classes, and other activities aimed at new mums. I'd walk for miles to attend a 'mother and baby' session, where I'd sip coffee and refuse cake. I attended every activity going, to help give my baby the best start in life...from baby yoga and massage, to music, crafts and breastfeeding groups. I put as much effort into my daughter's development as I did to my career.

I started adding in work to my schedule. I'd walk with the pushchair in one hand and my mobile phone in the other. I felt stressed, exhausted, fragile and fat.

I worked hard at my media business and equally hard at attachment parenting. I tried my best to be a 'miracle' mother, whilst juggling everything and living at Richard's parents' house.

When I took Jasmine to baby groups I'd try and focus on her, but I'd be thinking about work and everything I had to do. I'd look at all the other mums cooing over their kids, whilst I'd be panicking about getting more work and earning more money so that we could move into our own home.

A lot of the other mums were older and more settled; they seemed to have it together. I hadn't even established my career yet. I didn't have a stable home or relationship. I was just making do.

So much of my life was up in the air. I missed my friends and family in Sheffield. The only familiar thing I had was the bully inside me. She gave me comfort when I felt uncomfortable. She was my friend when I felt isolated. She gave me certainty during uncertainty. She offered a distraction whenever I felt pain.

CHAPTER
THIRTEEN

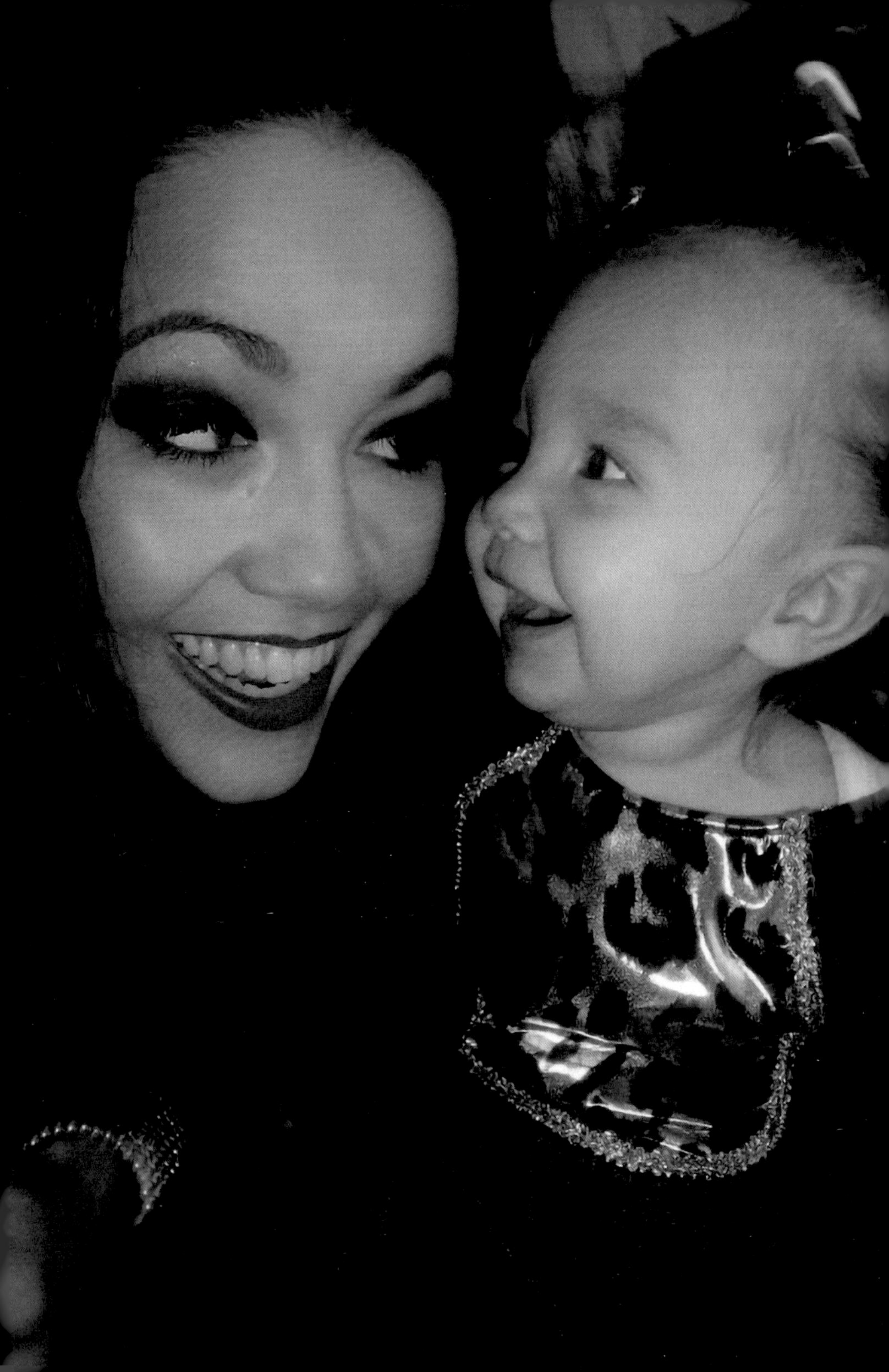

'You gotta make your own kind of music, sing your own special song.
Make your own kind of music, even if nobody else sings along.'
~ Mama Cass, The Mamas and Papas

A couple of months after having Jasmine, I lost control of my life again. Weight had begun to drop off me; physical evidence that I was using my old coping mechanisms.

I struggled, living in someone else's house, trying to keep a baby quiet, trying to play by someone else's rules. I could feel my mind and my identity slipping away from me.

I was trying to work, to find my way as a new mother, trying to breastfeed, to co-sleep, to make friends, to discover a new area, to keep in touch with friends and family who weren't local. I tried to keep fit, I tried to diet…I was trying to spin too many plates. I didn't know which one to stop spinning as it felt as if they'd all come crashing down on me.

Everyone around me made suggestions or shared their opinions as to what I should and shouldn't be doing.

'Co-sleeping is great!'

'Don't co-sleep, you'll kill your baby.'

'Breastfeeding? You're creating a rod for your own back.'

'Working? Focus on being a mother.'

'Go back to work. We'll have the baby.'

'You've lost too much weight.'

'You look amazing. How did you lose the weight?'

I had so many mixed messages directed at me. I was new to motherhood and relatively new to my career…I felt like I had everything, yet I had nothing.

I felt a failure.

I'd visit family and friends in Sheffield, but I'd rarely allow myself to sit with them. I had to be on the move because if I wasn't, I'd crash.

Trekking up and down the seven hills of Sheffield, the busy traffic rushing past me, I pushed the running buggy further forward. I would not cave in. I felt physically weak, my blood sugar had dropped, and I was physically trembling, but I would not stop walking until I reached my destination.

I would not allow myself a rest, to get on a bus or hail a taxi. It wasn't to save money or the environment, if I'm being totally honest, it was to save me from the guilt that I hadn't done what I'd set out to do that day.

I'd walk five miles across some of the steepest hills in the city to meet a friend, then afterwards, walk back to my mum's. My friend and I would meet in a coffee shop near her home; the ten-mile round trip was my punishment for sitting down for an hour and drinking sweet cappuccinos.

At times, Jasmine wanted to feed, which was fine because I could put her in a sling and feed and walk, or I'd just jog faster to my destination.

As ever, I neglected my own health. I didn't eat enough. I didn't sleep enough. I'd set my goals for the day and I'd achieve them no matter what.

To some, my stubborn determination may be enviable. I just know my mind becomes so focused, so absolutely rigid, that I would have crumbled had I not met my goals that day. It's one of the great things about my personality, but also one of the most damaging elements.

I cut out food groups to get a grasp over my body, which had obviously changed during pregnancy and with breastfeeding. I busied my lonely mind with work and looked for courses to further my education. I discovered ways I could add value to the world, from volunteering for charity magazines to blogging about mental health, breastfeeding and parenting.

I thought that my home life would be more manageable if Jasmine and I attended lots of play groups, if I helped out at community groups, and if — when we were in the house — I just stayed in one small space with my baby, breastfeeding, doing my work or exercising.

I didn't factor in any time for my mental health appointments, or any downtime. I never switched off my devices or gave myself space to just be me. The big problem there: I didn't actually know who I was.

I wanted to be the best mum possible, as I felt so much guilt about not being in the 'perfect' situation—we were still living with our baby in a room at Richard's parents' house. I'd lost a lot of my media work. I'd paused my belly-dancing work. I even felt that I'd let my body go.

My outlet was the online world. I didn't fit in with most mums. The groups I went to were mainly full of working mums, but they were all upper-middle class. Most were in loving marriages and had stable homes (at least it appeared that way). They'd planned and prepared for their new lives as mothers—it was their everything. They'd discuss the amount of salt in stock cubes or the levels of fluoride in water.

I was simply trying to survive. I claimed benefits, as my freelance work was on hold; I was more bothered about getting my free milk, vegetable and vitamin vouchers than I was about checking the ingredients of everything.

Being younger than most mums, being from a poorer background, and being in an unstable relationship and a new area made me feel alienated. I struggled with my mental health.

I felt like I was in a glass bubble. I was in a dream world with an amazing baby, yet I just didn't fit in anywhere.

Health professionals tried to offer advice, but that just made matters worse. I was already my own worst enemy. I already hated myself enough. I already knew that, throughout all the aspects of my life, I wasn't enough.

I'd always looked externally for redemption, and often, my open heart led to people taking advantage of me. I struggled to understand what a positive relationship was. I craved to be loved, to feel fulfilled, for someone to make me whole.

I desperately searched for stability, something I'd never had.

My little family was amid a middle-class area—a contrast from where I was brought up. It had a local cricket club where all the women spent their weekends making teas and doting on their husbands as they played. Was that stability or subservience?

Maybe I could train myself to be a housewife. I envied those women's patience, their apparent lack of career ambition. I envied their normality. But I couldn't help who I was.

Perhaps if I did as I was told — gave up my work and lost my ambition — I could be a full-time, stay-at-home mum. I could look after our home…well, our cramped bedroom in someone else's house.

I felt my energy and sense of self depleting. As my baby sucked at my breast, draining me of milk, I was tired, low in energy, and my mood was rock bottom. The only thing I felt I could do well was breastfeed. Regardless of my financial situation, where we lived or the strength of my relationship with her father, that was the one thing I could give Jasmine. Yet I was constantly criticised about that, too.

I'd loved the health visitor I had in Sheffield, where my pregnancy journey began. She was also working class, the salt of the earth. She'd say, 'If you want to whack your boob out to feed your baby, do it. If you don't, and you want to bottle-feed, do that. My main concern is your health, which will impact the baby, too.' Now I lived within a different funding body.

Eventually, as is often said, you 'find your people'…it just took me a while to find groups where I felt relaxed and at ease. I attended Bosom Buddies, which was led by a local breastfeeding charity. They came to where I lived and gave me down-to-earth breastfeeding support. I also received help from a charity that supported vulnerable families, called Homestart. I found more groups at local churches that were great as well as a few others that met at fantastic coffee shops.

Labels are strange. On my human rights blog and in documentaries I'd reported on people in similar situations to the one I was in. I'd talked about their struggles, and now here I was, trying to navigate the welfare system myself and being classed as 'vulnerable'.

Now that I'd started to make some friends and I'd become familiar with my home city of Wakefield, I used the time I spent walking or jogging to research story ideas for documentaries. I also explored the requirements for a qualification in journalism.

Around this time, I met a fellow female film-maker, Daria, in

a coffee shop. We hit it off straightaway. The opposite of me —
calm, steady and logical — she didn't have kids, but she totally
accepted that, at every meeting, I'd have Jasmine in the sling,
feeding.

Daria wasn't fazed by anything and she had all the skills I
lacked, such as a love of the technical and for production. She
didn't have contacts or a creative mind, nor a desire to be on
camera. It seemed natural to work together on documentaries
that fuelled our shared passion of giving a voice to people who
had been ignored or who were unheard.

Time at home was largely spent breastfeeding. When Jasmine
slept in her bouncer, I worked at Richard's small desk in his
bedroom. My research brought the Journalism Diversity Fund
to my attention; I applied for a grant to pay for post-graduate
diploma studies at the University of Salford.

I had my sights set on Salford, as that was where MediaCity
UK was based, the new home of the BBC in the North. Despite
what would be a two-hour commute from Wakefield, I thought
it would be worth it — not just to obtain my qualification, but for
Daria and me to establish useful contacts.

At the same time, our little family moved into our own place.
We considered Salford, but we could get an entire house in
Wakefield for the same price as renting a flat near the university.
I decided that I'd commute to Salford when I absolutely had to
be at university, with Jasmine in the nursery at MediaCity on
those days.

On autopilot, I got our little family ready to move into our new
home, I embarked on a new qualification and a new business,
and I had to deal with leaving Jasmine for the first time, despite
still breastfeeding her.

I thought returning to university would be positive stimulation
for my brain as well as something in my life that would be
mine. But it felt weird, adapting to uni life once again, with the
responsibilities, perhaps, of someone a lot older.

I wanted to make friends, but at the same time, it was hard
as my priorities were totally different. Because I'd worked in

journalism for a while by then, it felt like I'd gone backwards. I was annoyed at myself and frustrated because I wasn't fulfilling any of my roles very well.

Some mornings, I had to get up at 4 a.m. to get myself and the baby ready before commuting in rush hour traffic. I then had to peel Jasmine off me and put her in nursery, before making the ten-minute walk further into the media hubbub of the North — where, supposedly, my dreams lay. In actual fact, I spent my days either in lectures or trying to pump breast milk for Jasmine in one of the glass-walled studios.

I had no time or headspace to socialise, which wasn't important, as all I wanted to do was get back to my baby; we were together in the car, even if it was during stressful commutes.

I lived at such a fast pace that I didn't even make the most of being in MediaCity, as I was always rushing in or out. I began to feel the stress overwhelm me from different pressures: studying, nursing a young baby, commuting, moving house, and also trying to make money…either through bits of freelance work for national news, or as a belly-dancer in restaurants.

I was still passionate about business and 'giving back', so I took on extra courses to learn more about growing a social enterprise. I didn't have any direction, just passion and a crumbling mind.

On a few occasions, I could feel myself on the verge of another breakdown. It got to the point where I'd pull up at the side of the road and question everything — such as why I made such an arduous, physical journey all the time. Why I always found myself on an emotional rollercoaster.

I began to find driving stressful. On the way to an examination, to determine if I was dyslexic or had dyspraxia, I literally stopped the car in the middle of the road. I couldn't find where I was going, and I'd been driving round in circles for ages. I'd been up since 4 a.m., I'd managed to get my daughter in nursery…this was supposed to be my time to work on myself, and all I was doing was pushing myself over the edge.

To the outside world, I may have looked like I had it all. A baby, a new home, a boyfriend; studying for an MA, freelance work at the Daily Mirror and local newspapers, together with a flourishing career as a belly-dancer.

I felt like I had nothing. And that I was letting my child down – the most important person in my life. I didn't have the answer or a way out.

I was eventually diagnosed with both dyslexia and dyspraxia, which really helped me to understand myself. It explained why I found driving, learning shorthand, and organisation difficult.

It was why I over-committed and would do anything rather than let other people down. I was the ultimate people-pleaser, yet the only person I was disappointing was myself.

One night, after finishing a course on social entrepreneurship in Liverpool, I was due to see my friend in Manchester for her birthday. I'd arranged to stay the night on another friend's sofa before going into work at the Daily Mirror on the outskirts of Manchester the following day.

After the course finished, I quickly got changed into the first 'going out' outfit I'd worn since giving birth. I was a little nervous, as I hadn't socialised with the group before; I was always rushing to the nursery to collect Jasmine or trying to cram in all my work. I wasn't even sure what I had to talk about with people anymore.

As I drove along the motorway from Liverpool to Manchester, I struggled to hold on to the steering wheel. It was dark and raining heavily. I began to panic – I was already late for the party, but I needed to concentrate on my driving in such treacherous conditions.

I felt the wheels of the car turn of their own accord and I lost control of the steering wheel. The next thing I remember was spinning in the middle of the motorway. It was like I was in a real-life version of dodgems at the fair.

It came to a halt in the opposite direction. Cars sped past me. Luckily, a couple of them stopped to help me. They called the police and the ambulance service.

On the stretcher, as my clothes were cut away, I remember

panicking when they asked who they should call. 'Please don't call my boyfriend, it's his and his dad's car as well as mine. Please, I'm going to be in so much trouble!' I asked them instead if they would text my workplace, to say that I'd be late in the following day.

The paramedics laughed. 'There's no way you're going in to work!'

I couldn't even think about my injuries. I'd let my boyfriend down, let my work down, let down the friends I was supposed to be meeting. I didn't even have a clue how I would get home to my baby.

*

I somehow fudged my way through to the end of my post-graduate diploma. I still felt like I was letting everyone down, that I'd taken on way too much. I didn't feel like I was doing anything well.

I was surprised but delighted that the investigative radio documentary I'd made with Daria in my spare time whilst at university — via our company, Evoke Media Group — had been nominated for three awards: a national journalism award, a national commercial radio award, and one from the university.

I don't know why I always struggled to compete with others on a small scale, yet I could seemingly give larger organisations a run for their money. In the end, our documentary was highly commended in the university award, highly commended in the national commercial radio awards (against some of the biggest radio stations in the UK) and it achieved 'scoop of the year' in the national journalism awards.

The only way I was able to attend the national journalism awards was if I took Jasmine with me in the sling; this caused cooing from some of the guests and a good dose of judgement from others, but there was no way I could leave her to travel down South for the weekend, because she fed so often.

Rather than enjoy a rest after my journalism studies, I set my sights on building and promoting Evoke and making our own documentaries. I explored every avenue for funding, to support our mission as female film-makers in the North, who were passionate about subjects such as poverty and mental health. Anything I set my mind to, I could do it.

I was invited to speak across the globe on entrepreneurship and social affairs, but this meant I was constantly torn between work and the time spent with my daughter and feeding her myself. I gave up some once-in-a-lifetime opportunities, because I couldn't, and wouldn't, leave Jasmine for more than a couple of nights, maximum.

However, I did take the opportunity to report on a technology event in Barcelona. Once I was in the zone, I was fine and I'd manage to secure the big celebrity interviews no one else could. But the anxiety that built up before I went away was enormous. I'd also compensate for my absence by shopping excessively, buying 'guilt gifts' for my daughter.

I conceded that I should only apply for opportunities close to home in future.

I felt a bit of a joke. I kept touching the kind of 'success' people told me about, but I wouldn't be able to see it through. I loved dreaming about all the possibilities with my career, and I even enjoyed interviews, but when I got the award, grant or position, I'd panic and become overwhelmed with imposter syndrome. On the flipside, bosses and decision-makers loved me initially, because I helped them tick a lot of boxes, but once the opportunity was underway, they'd try and mould me, so that I fit in with the status quo. I could do this temporarily, being a people pleaser, then my mask would slip, and I'd have to really force myself to do things that I didn't believe in or I wasn't passionate about.

I managed, over thousands of other applicants, to be accepted onto a Journalism Trainee Scheme run by the BBC. I'd applied to other schemes, but I was too qualified, too experienced or not experienced enough for a staff job. I was adamant that I wanted to stay in the North and live at home.

The BBC opportunity felt like a dream come true – paid training and placements on The One Show, and BBC Radio 4 in

Salford. Despite my joy at securing the placement, it felt weird to be a trainee again. I'd done everything back to front, I'd already worked at local BBC stations, on national news, on local news, then gone back to study journalism — and now I was a trainee!

All that said, I felt the scheme 'got me'; though I'd scored quite low on my spelling and grammar tests in the initial application, I'd achieved the highest scores in my interview for my story ideas, originality and teamwork. I was actually ecstatic to have the opportunity to start again and use the plethora of ideas I had.

But life had another plan for me. During the induction process I discovered I was pregnant again. It wasn't planned, though it wasn't as much of a shock as my first pregnancy had been. I felt awful, as some of the BBC bosses had taken a chance on me. I felt like I'd let them down.

I began working out how I could continue until I gave birth. I was gutted in many ways, as I had to postpone a lot of other work opportunities; however, I was also ecstatic to be having another baby — and an enforced break from my career ambitions.

This pregnancy was different. Rather than boosting my mental health and aiding my recovery from my eating disorder, it proved the opposite. Maybe I was fatigued from starting a new job, with a young child already, or it was the result of a completely different mix of emotions and hormones.

Maybe there was no explanation for what I was about to experience.

CHAPTER FOURTEEN

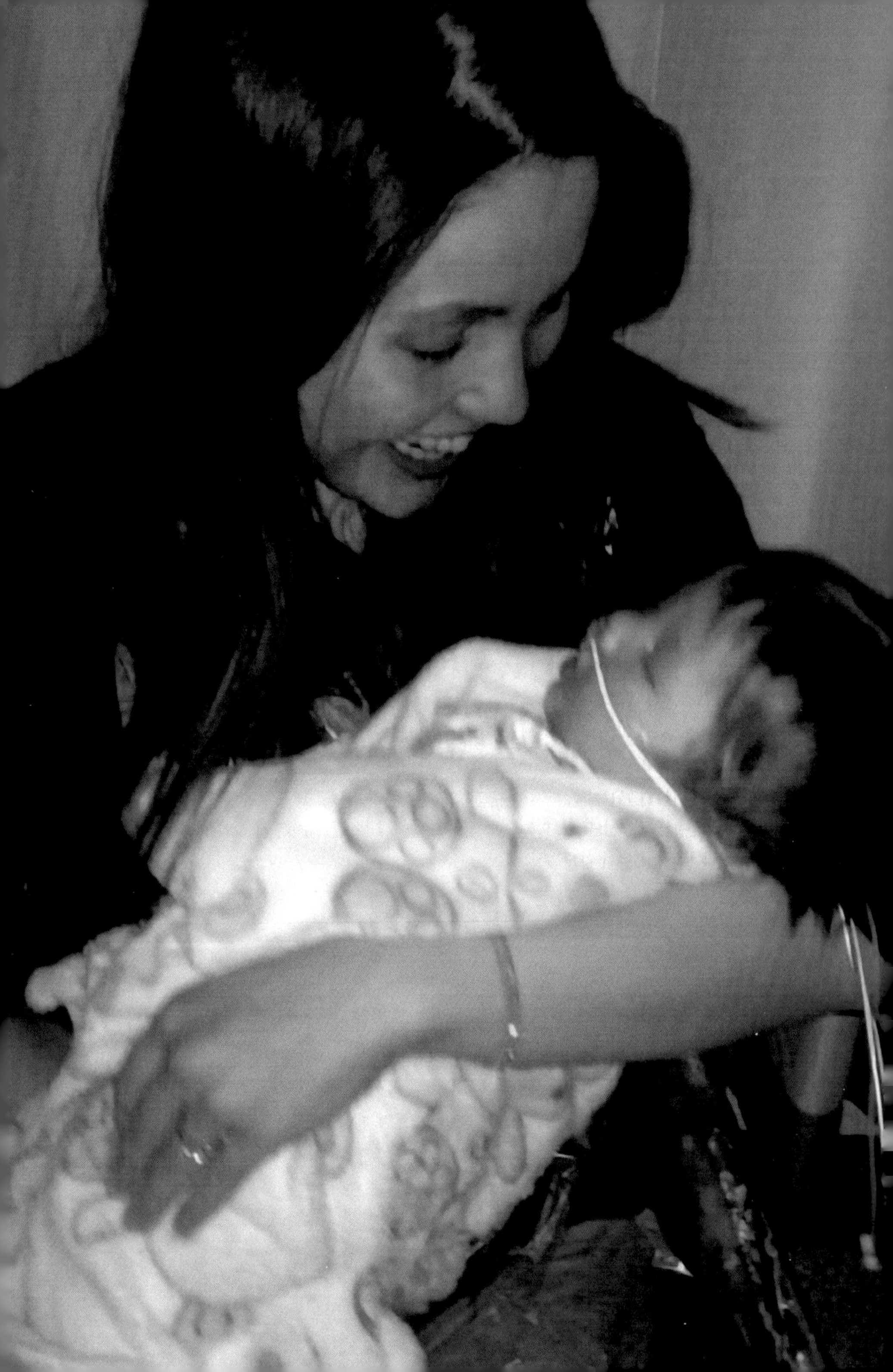

'It is health that is real wealth and not pieces of gold and silver.'
~ Mahatma Gandhi

For as long as I can remember I've experienced distressing episodes of what I can only describe as 'loudness' — where my mind races, my body freezes, and I struggle to distinguish what is real and what isn't real.

I hear and see things that, I'm told, aren't there.

The worst period of my life, mentally, was when everything seemed to be going well.

It was the winter of 2014. I was seven months pregnant with my second child and looking after two-year-old Jasmine when I had my first psychotic episode.

Jasmine was asleep in her bed. As I lay next to her, I thought the walls were caving in. Richard was on a night out. I was so scared. I felt sick and dizzy as the room began to shake.

I checked on my phone for reports of an earthquake, but I couldn't find anything. I peeked through the curtains to see if anybody was trying to destroy our house and capture us. I visualised our escape route out of the bedroom windows should the attackers come from downstairs.

I couldn't see anything, but I knew they were there, somewhere. I blockaded the bedroom door in an attempt to keep us safe. I peeked again through the curtains. I was sure I saw something outside…eyes watching our house from behind the trees. We were under attack; it would happen at any moment.

My heart raced, my mind whirred and my palms began to sweat.

We remained like that for hours: I constantly checked the room and peered through the windows then I'd scroll through my phone whilst Jasmine slept beside me. Eventually, my medication kicked in and, despite the adrenaline rushing through my body, my eyes closed.

*

A few days later, my mind calm, I felt there may be some truth in what my mental health nurse had been saying for a while — that I was paranoid and suffering from psychosis.

Having been diagnosed with depression and an eating disorder when I was just twelve years-old, a lot of health professionals were already involved in my care — with greater focus during my pregnancies.

However, nearly all the extra appointments I had just focused on my physical health — or at the very best I was asked to complete tick-box surveys on how I felt. The doctors also asked closed questions to cover their backs.

'You're not suicidal, are you? You look fine to me.'

'You won't self-harm, will you?'

'You're not thinking of hurting anyone, right?'

Fortunately, at a routine antenatal appointment, a consultant obstetrician had the initiative to check my mental health. He asked open questions and listened to my responses. Finally, my mental health care escalated.

I was scared, but it also gave me a glimmer of hope. Maybe I was mentally ill, and life didn't always have to feel this bad?

Maybe people weren't after me.

I had various check-ups with nurses, psychiatrists and psychologists, who discussed the best avenue for me, e.g. inpatient care or more intensive care in the community. They decided to assess me inside a mental health hospital in Wakefield.

As I drove through the barrier of the unit, tears welled in my eyes. The walls of the high-security hospital looked bland, dark and scary; they loomed over the driveway and sported barbed wire across the top. It looked like a prison.

Except this was much worse than a prison. At least in prison you had a release date or a predetermined sentence.

I felt I didn't deserve help. I had a family, a fiancé, a job and another baby on the way. My life looked good to the outside world.

I felt out of place there. I didn't look or sound mad (however 'madness' looks or sounds), I was just me.

I was in an excruciatingly dark, lonely place. I thought the professionals — regardless of their role in the NHS or how posh they sounded — were trying to interfere with my life. They couldn't see or hear what was going on inside my mind, so how were they qualified to help me?

I thought there was a conspiracy against me. That people were after me and my unborn baby. I remember sitting with a psychiatrist and being so very careful of what I said, because my attackers were watching. As I sat in the bare room, decorated only with old office chairs and the table we were sat around, the voices became louder.

I tried to block them out. I began to whisper to the psychiatrist in a bid to prevent the attackers from hearing. The voices became louder still, deafening my soft replies.

'You're lying,' they said. 'Just keep quiet, you're a liar.'

Was I lying? Were the voices real? Was the psychiatrist even real? Who could I trust?

After a lengthy and emotionally draining assessment I was eventually diagnosed with psychosis, an acute psychotic disorder. The term sounded scary. Maybe I was mad after all.

I struggled to believe I had a mental illness. I was scared that the professionals hadn't realised what was actually going on, and that I was still under attack.

I was given the option of being admitted to a mother and baby unit for specialist support or being cared for at home. We decided it was best to try and keep me at home; I couldn't bear to be away from Jasmine, and I didn't want to give birth to my second baby in a hospital far away.

I received crisis care support, which consisted of daily visits from community mental health nurses, who would talk to me and make sure I took my medication. I hated having to welcome a new person into my home each day; whilst they were always friendly, I found a lot of their comments patronising. 'But you're so pretty. You've got so much going for you...'

Finally, after months of trialling various antipsychotic drugs, I began to feel more stable and the voices became quieter.

During that time, I'd been advised to write down how I was feeling, which I enjoyed. I find writing a good way to express myself. During bad psychotic episodes, however, when I would roll around on the floor, believing someone was shooting at me, my enthusiasm for writing was not there. I could barely sit down, let alone write about what I was experiencing. It was very real to me at the time—I genuinely thought I was under attack and people were out to get me.

Once things were more manageable and the medication kicked in, I kept a video diary of my progress on my phone. I was still in the midst of psychosis, but at least I had an outlet to express myself where I was not being judged.

The more I documented my journey, the easier it became to talk about it. I could verbalise what I was going through to the camera, even when I couldn't find the right words for my journal or when speaking to professionals.

Vlogging became a form of therapy in its own right. It was there for me in my good moments and my bad ones. I didn't have to put on a happy face and make a cup of tea for it or tidy my house in preparation, like I felt I had to do when medics visited my home. I could just do it.

It was an effective tool for me to reflect on my progress. Recovery in any form is a weird spinning wheel...even if it's going in the right direction, it's hard to recognise that when it's actually happening.

I began sharing what I'd been through on social media—as I hate that pictures can be used to show a curated side of someone's life. I felt it was important to be open and honest about what really went on behind the scenes of someone who looked like they had it all.

Whilst many people were shocked by the reality I showed, I received messages from similarly ambitious women who also struggled. Leaders, mothers, celebrities, friends, colleagues...so many women who I assumed had 'their shit together' were also trapped in the success cycle.

Their reactions encouraged me to share more of my story. There's still a stigma around mental health—not just within society, but how we judge ourselves. However, I felt it important to talk candidly about the stark reality of mental health problems, rather than just using the words, 'I feel so anxious/depressed.'

No job title, background or career success makes you immune from mental health problems; in fact, I began to realise that 'success' and the pressure to have it all at any cost, can be a huge part of the problem.

I vowed to make the most of my skills as a journalist and my life experiences to help others. It gave me a purpose whilst I rediscovered my identity. I felt that this was my calling.

*

I had a relatively smooth birth the second time around. I took some maternity leave so I could prepare, and I even created a labour playlist. No whale music for me, just pure R&B and belly-dancing music!

Unlike the time before, when I'd blindly gone along with the health professionals during induction and giving birth, I attended a Birth Choices group; they empowered me to uphold my birth plan and to be assertive over how I wanted things to unfold. They also told me what I needed to do if I felt control was being taken from me.

Sometimes, things don't go to plan — like the water pool being broken, which meant I couldn't use it. Overall, though, I ensured my choices were implemented, such as delayed cord clamping, using only gas and air, and having as much skin to skin contact with my baby as I wanted. It made me realise how traumatic it can be to not have choices over your body and birth; that medics prodding and poking you is not always a necessity.

Following Arianna's birth, we all settled at home. I managed to be kinder to myself and I gave myself a couple of days 'off' — I didn't try to exercise, and we didn't have any other visitors than those I wanted.

My mental health was rocky, but nowhere near as bad as it had been after Jasmine's birth. I looked back at some of the footage I'd recorded at that time and I couldn't believe how poorly I'd been, or how rough I looked.

At baby groups, I realised that many other mums were struggling with their mental health. And whilst people were being increasingly open about it, there still wasn't the support available.

Campaigns encouraged those suffering to talk, which is a good thing — but where was the support for mums before things went too far, like they had with me? The campaigner-cum-journalist within me started researching. I discovered how few places existed that helped mums, even when they were at crisis point. And how many mums were scared to speak too openly, for fear of having their children taken away from them. This actually happened to some mothers.

I started to feel the fire inside me burn. I had to do something. I decided to share my videos with an editor I knew at the BBC. Granted, in my vlog, I didn't look 'professional' or like a typical BBC journalist, but this was much more important than my vanity.

With the vlogs covering my personal journey, and the films Daria and I had made under Evoke, we had enough footage for a documentary. The BBC aired it with the title 'Mad Mums'.

It's funny how life takes you in one direction then throws you off course into another. Making the documentary gave me the confidence to return to more positive coping mechanisms, like dance and drama. I even played football for the first time in years. I began to run again, with Arianna in the buggy.

I realised that, even though I wasn't the finished product, my journey to a healthier life could help others a few steps behind me.

My next challenge was not related to my own health, but my baby's. It was a normal Sunday. I took Jasmine to play football and carried Arianna in the sling. It was ideal for me; I could stand on the side-lines and watch Jasmine play whilst Arianna nestled into my chest and fed from me, before she fell asleep, content.

After football, I took the girls to the local art gallery. I loved to keep them stimulated whilst being out and about, and it was good for my own mental health, too. As we entered the gallery's automatic doors, I felt Arianna slump inside the sling. I looked down and her head was floppy and her face, grey. My heart thumped against my chest. I untied the sling and ran, with the lifeless body of my baby, to the reception desk.

She wasn't breathing. The only evidence of life I could see was blood trickling from her nose and around her mouth.

Was this really happening? Was my baby dead?

I urged the receptionist, 'Call an ambulance. Please call an ambulance. She's not breathing!'

The woman looked shocked. She paused for a moment before picking up the phone.

I leant Arianna on the side of the desk. Her body was still. I picked her up again and started to gently rub her chest and rock her, as if trying to wake her up…as if trying to spark some life into her.

She still didn't move. She still wasn't breathing.

An onlooker spotted the commotion and rushed over. 'Are you okay?' he asked.

'No! My baby's not breathing,' I screamed.

The next moments are a blur. I remember laying Arianna on the cold, grey concrete floor of the gallery's entrance hall. The stranger somehow managed to calm me down so that we could attempt to resuscitate her. I remembered a BBC radio documentary I'd listened to during my journalism training, where a baby had stopped breathing and its mum had called 999, who described, step by step, how to administer CPR.

Usually, in a crisis, everything happens at breakneck speed, but every second Arianna failed to breathe felt like an hour. I'm not even sure I breathed in those moments.

I felt Jasmine next to me. She was only three years-old; somehow, she knew to remain quiet and stay close.

After what felt like an eternity, a first responder arrived. They asked a lot of questions and began checking Arianna. Shortly after, two paramedics rushed in. They ventilated her and I can't describe the relief I felt when I saw her chest finally move.

She took a laboured breath. Things were still touch and go.

Arianna was taken on a stretcher into the ambulance waiting outside. Paramedics guided Jasmine and I to sit by her side and they managed to look after all three of us.

I was in shock. Jasmine needed distracting, and Arianna was still only breathing with the assistance of a ventilator.

My baby girl was rushed into the emergency suite of the local hospital, the same hospital in which she'd been born. I didn't dare think about it...her place of birth could also become her place of death.

A team of doctors and nurses swarmed the room and started to resuscitate her. I was ushered away. I desperately didn't want to let go of Arianna, but I also knew I had to let the medical team do what they'd been trained to do.

The child I'd given life to, the child that had been attached to me, the child I'd fed and nurtured was now separated from me. I could no longer help her. I had to let her go.

Richard arrived with his parents, who looked after Jasmine. We waited anxiously in the family room. I still had my changing bag with me, full of snacks, wipes, muslin cloths, nappies and my purse. I thought I had everything I needed for the day...how wrong was I? Who needs healthy snacks or wipes when their baby isn't even able to breathe?

The medics successfully ventilated Arianna, but she still wasn't able to breathe on her own — and they didn't know why.

It was suggested that she may have suffocated in the sling. My heart almost stopped when they said that. Had I killed her? Had I smothered my own flesh and blood?

Arianna was transported from Pinderfields Hospital in Wakefield to Leeds General Infirmary, so that she could be treated in their Paediatric Intensive Care Unit.

I asked every doctor, every medical professional, and anyone involved in Arianna's care, 'Will she be okay? Will she? Please tell me she'll be okay.'

No one could reassure me. She was struggling, even with the ventilator and hooked up to various machines. Her body looked tiny on the huge hospital bed, with just plastic for protection.

I couldn't hug her. I couldn't hold her. I couldn't feed her. I could only pray for her and express milk, hoping that one day she'd be able to drink it.

All we could do was put our trust in the doctors and nurses, the consultants, and the wider world. I reached out on social media, begging people to pray for her.

There was also the worry that she'd suffered brain damage from a lack of oxygen. I just clung to the hope that she'd survive, no matter what.

I remember telling myself that, if Arianna died, I would, too. I was riddled with guilt. I'd read about the power of 'babywearing' in my attachment parenting books, but there was no mention of any suffocation risk.

As the hours passed, Arianna's small, frail body still wasn't able to breathe unaided. My prayers weren't being answered. I focused on expressing as much milk as I could and I also started a video diary. I couldn't write about those dark moments — my brain was too foggy.

I shut myself away in the family room, which I had to myself to express milk. I didn't want to communicate with anyone other than the hospital staff. I occasionally went for a walk, but rather than this providing a break from the hospital and some mental clarity, I spent the time planning how to take my own life.

Not long after, a doctor came to find me. Something was wrong. He explained that they needed to insert a tracheostomy into Arianna's throat. This would help to ventilate her, but it could also kill her. She still wasn't breathing properly; they needed to do it.

The baby I'd carefully rocked, carried, clothed and fed was about to have her throat slit open. And I wasn't allowed to touch her or be in the room when it happened.

In that moment I dropped to my knees, wailing, praying. Surely, this was a surreal movie I was trapped in. I trusted the staff, they were incredible; now I had to have faith that this nightmare would soon be over.

As I crumbled, the doctor returned with news. Just as they were about to cut into Arianna's tiny, delicate neck, she'd taken a breath...her first breath since her ordeal began.

She no longer needed a tracheostomy.

Had that moment not changed my life and my perspective about what was truly important, I don't know what would have. Work, home, money...nothing is as important as our health.

As quickly as things had spiralled downwards, they started to escalate upwards. Just the next day I was able to hold Arianna. She was still covered in tubes, but the nurses who had loved her back to life knew that I needed to hold my baby. The only connection we'd had since arriving at hospital was a muslin blanket the hospital had given me to hold, which was placed near Arianna as she'd fought for her life.

As my baby went from strength to strength, the doctors were able to tell me what had happened to her, and why she'd deteriorated so quickly. The consultant explained that the sling had probably saved Arianna's life, in that I'd been able to feel her go limp. She had streptococcal bacteria (Strep B) and pneumonia; because she was so young, her body had just shut down. Had she been in a pram or a cot she would almost certainly have died, as I probably wouldn't have noticed her condition soon enough to resuscitate her.

Miraculously, Arianna suffered no brain damage, nor was she left with any ongoing health issues; however, time will tell whether this remains the case.

Eventually, she was transferred to the children's unit in Pinderfields, then allowed home to be cared for in the community.

*

Whilst focusing on my baby's illness, I left my dream job in the media. I needed time out to recover and focus on my family, as well as regain some confidence. I needed to find my identity now that I wasn't reacting to yet another crisis.

It's hard to change careers and go against what people think you should do. But, after experiencing what I'd experienced in the last few years alone, it seemed natural to reflect and refocus my ambition.

During moments where you want to die, or when a loved one nearly dies, you don't count how many awards you've won or how many followers you have online – you go back to basics.

I began to think about loved ones in my life, and the time I'd wasted worrying about work and my career. I couldn't have cared less about the money I earned or lost…life had shown me what was important: love, my values and my relationships.

When Arianna was ill, I promised myself that, if she survived, things would be different. I would not return to the life I had before her illness. I'd changed. My perspective on life had changed.

Would I care about getting the top story on the national news, if I felt suicidal and would rather die than suffer any longer with the pain?

Would I care that I'd invested so much time and money into being an international businesswoman, dancer and journalist, if it meant being away from my kids?

Would I actually care whether I met that deadline if I didn't have my health?

Health is wealth. Without health, we don't have wealth.

I visualised my values as giant marbles; I placed them in a metaphorical jar, then added in all the little marbles that represented other aspects of my life.

Once I knew my 'why', I could see how insignificant many of my career goals were. They were just little marbles. Too often, I placed so many of these into my 'jar' that the big marbles couldn't get in. As a result, I'd lost my purpose, to the point that I visualised killing myself over what my future would look like. To the point where I fantasised about self-harming.

I knew I had to remain well, because I was the main carer for my daughters. This was my last chance.

I wasn't about to become a gushy, 'mumsy' mum—I was still ambitious. But my ambition now was to be content, fulfilled and to add value.

I created blogs and vlogs to help other mums and women like me. I took my time building my confidence in order to leave the house again—the tragic event, when my youngest had nearly died in my arms, was the last time I'd been on a solo outing with the kids.

I couldn't do it alone. I needed help, both personally and professionally. It takes, as they say, a village to raise a child. I was also painfully aware that no man (or woman) is an island.

CHAPTER
FIFTEEN

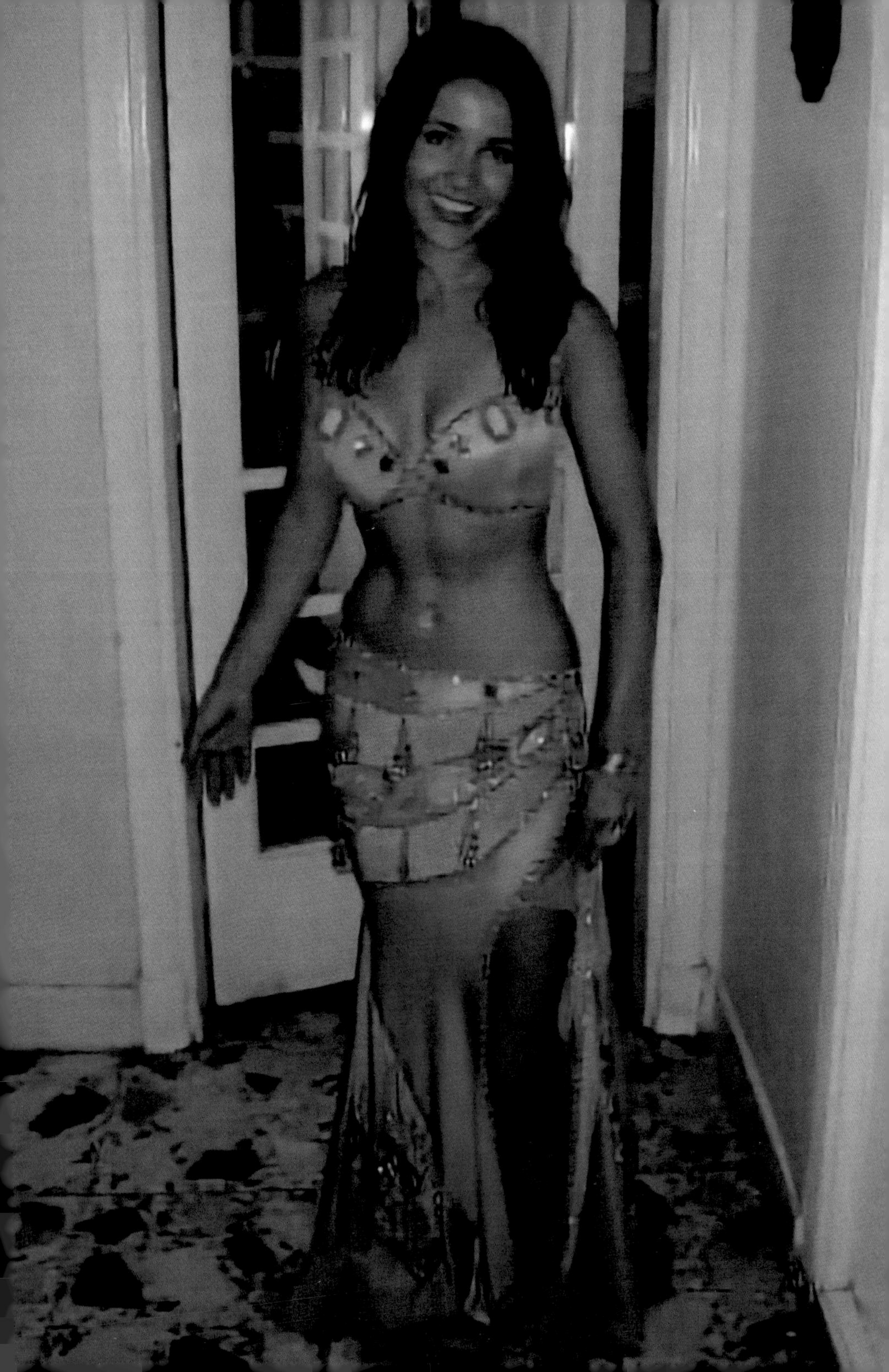

'Don't dream it, be it. Don't dream it, be it.
Don't dream it, be it. Don't dream it, be it.'
~ Rocky Horror Picture Show

I began my next mission: to build a community. A support network, to help myself and others thrive. People had always told me, 'It's not what you know, it's who you know.' It's a known fact that you become the five people you spend the most time with.

I never understood this, in terms of my career. It wasn't in my nature to make friends or acquaintances just to further my career or to make more money. Granted, networking is important, and knowing people in high places helps, but I'd got this far by just being myself.

My best work, such as my stories that made the news, had brought the biggest impact, and they hadn't come from schmoozing rich people in high places. They'd been the result of the time I'd spent with a range of communities, and because I genuinely cared about my fellow human beings.

My dance success stemmed from the time I spent at grassroots, in community belly-dancing groups at my local church hall, where I learnt the best of the art form. My stubbornness, determination and passion came from my challenging past and growing up in a poor area.

My sense of right and wrong developed from the injustice I'd experienced and the inequality and unfair treatment those around me had received.

I was now more concerned with being surrounded by people with big hearts and values that aligned with mine. I'd seen how shallow people could be…the people who only wanted to know me when I had my fifteen minutes of fame. People who'd neglected me when I was suffering the most.

We all need people around us who don't care what our societal status is, who don't care whether we have money or fame. People who see our hearts are the ones that will ultimately help you succeed in every aspect of life.

Children can also help you understand what's important. They're not bothered about titles or careers; they just want you to love and care for them. They value your time. My daughters helped to give me focus, and finally, I could see a future again, full of love and passion.

I invested my time in a range of people and groups, because one person or group can't fulfil every need. We must enjoy diverse relationships, to help us thrive physically, mentally, emotionally, spiritually and intellectually.

*

Charity befrienders eventually helped me leave the house. I didn't have the confidence to walk to the park across the road with the kids, let alone attend a therapy group. At times I was frustrated with myself...how had I gone from being a budding journalist at BBC News—reporting on stories like the one I was now living—to now being a case study for anxiety, depression and psychosis?

I'm only human. We're actually at our most beautiful when in our rawest state. Yes, it's nice to be able to say, 'I worked for BBC News/Channel 4 News/ITV News'. It was what I'd always dreamed of.

I just appreciated seeing the trees again...learning to play with my daughter...getting together with friends and mindfully sipping on a soya milk hot chocolate, whilst breastfeeding Arianna.

I started to enjoy the sweetness in my drink and looking at my baby suckling reminded me of what was important.

I still grieved for the career I lost, the one I thought made me happy. I poured my ambition into my blog and building up my YouTube channel, adding value my way. I didn't feel I belonged in most newsrooms, and I didn't have the strength to always be the minority—the token 'mixed race poor girl', the young mum or the 'rags to riches' story—just to tick diversity boxes.

At the same time, not being heard was exhausting and demoralising. I wanted to be me, and I wanted to make the media work for people like me.

After showing an editor the vlogs I'd made in intensive care as my daughter was loved back to life, they agreed to make them into another documentary; I wanted it to show my appreciation for the NHS. Expressing gratitude is one of the most powerful things we can do.

Rather than my initial thoughts of, 'Why my daughter? Why us?', when I had time to think in the hospital waiting room, I began to truly appreciate all I had in my life, and just how lucky I was to be living in a country where I didn't have to worry about paying for healthcare. Richard and I didn't have to choose what we could afford to save our daughter; we were all blessed, being in a country where the National Health Service is mostly funded.

Suddenly, my career goals transformed into a calling, which had much more value and purpose than any money or job title could have given me.

Friends, family and mental health professionals initially tried to encourage me to just take a break and not give up on my original career goals altogether. 'You can always go back to them,' they said. The truth was, I didn't want to. It would break me. I'd been reminded of what life was really about; in those environments it's hard to keep hold of what's important.

I started to attend church again. I went to playgroups where there were other mums like me—nothing you said shocked them. I went to 'high-brow' playgroups, too, when I wanted to talk about business, but it was definitely the simple, 'no frills' groups that helped. Despite our pasts, we were just happy to sit on the floor with a beaker of tea and chat, laugh and cry about our situations.

I invested in friendships that were unwavering. People who, no matter what, would be there for me whether I was rich or poor, strong or weak, and regardless of what I looked like.

I didn't have one specific friendship circle; instead, I had lots of direct relationships or I belonged to numerous groups where I could chat about abuse or reality TV, for example.

These non-judgemental networks helped me grow. They encouraged me to utilise my skills in writing and film-making, and to use my own experience of mental health problems to help others.

Others like me.

Other like you.

Others who are successful and who strive to be their best self, but who, at the same time, find their drive in the darkest of places.

This is how I found my place in the world. My unique identity. Having been judged in every way, having never fit in. Having achieved 'career success' but losing myself in the process.

I wanted to share my journey that took me to death's door, after giving in to the bully inside me.

I'd tried to be the best mum, the best student, the best journalist, the best belly-dancer, the best eating disorder patient...at times I'd achieved all of these things... but at what cost? That was no life. I'd had to strive to be my best self for me, not for other's opinions or status.

To be stronger, I had to be my authentic self. And I needed to surround myself with people who enabled me to do just that.

Without realising it, I'd created an online career that thrived on authenticity. Involving women like me — who didn't follow me because they thought I had my shit together, but because they related to me; they had also struggled, they'd achieved success, but they'd also come to the conclusion that fame and money are not that important in the grand scheme of things.

They strived to be their best selves. They were also round pegs trying to fit into square holes...that was what was beautiful about them. They felt imposter syndrome, and they were also on a journey of discovery towards true success, whatever that looked like for them.

They'd felt pain, poverty, discrimination. They'd experienced success, riches and material wealth. But they knew, deep down, that true wealth is health.

We are all perfectly imperfect.

CHAPTER SIXTEEN

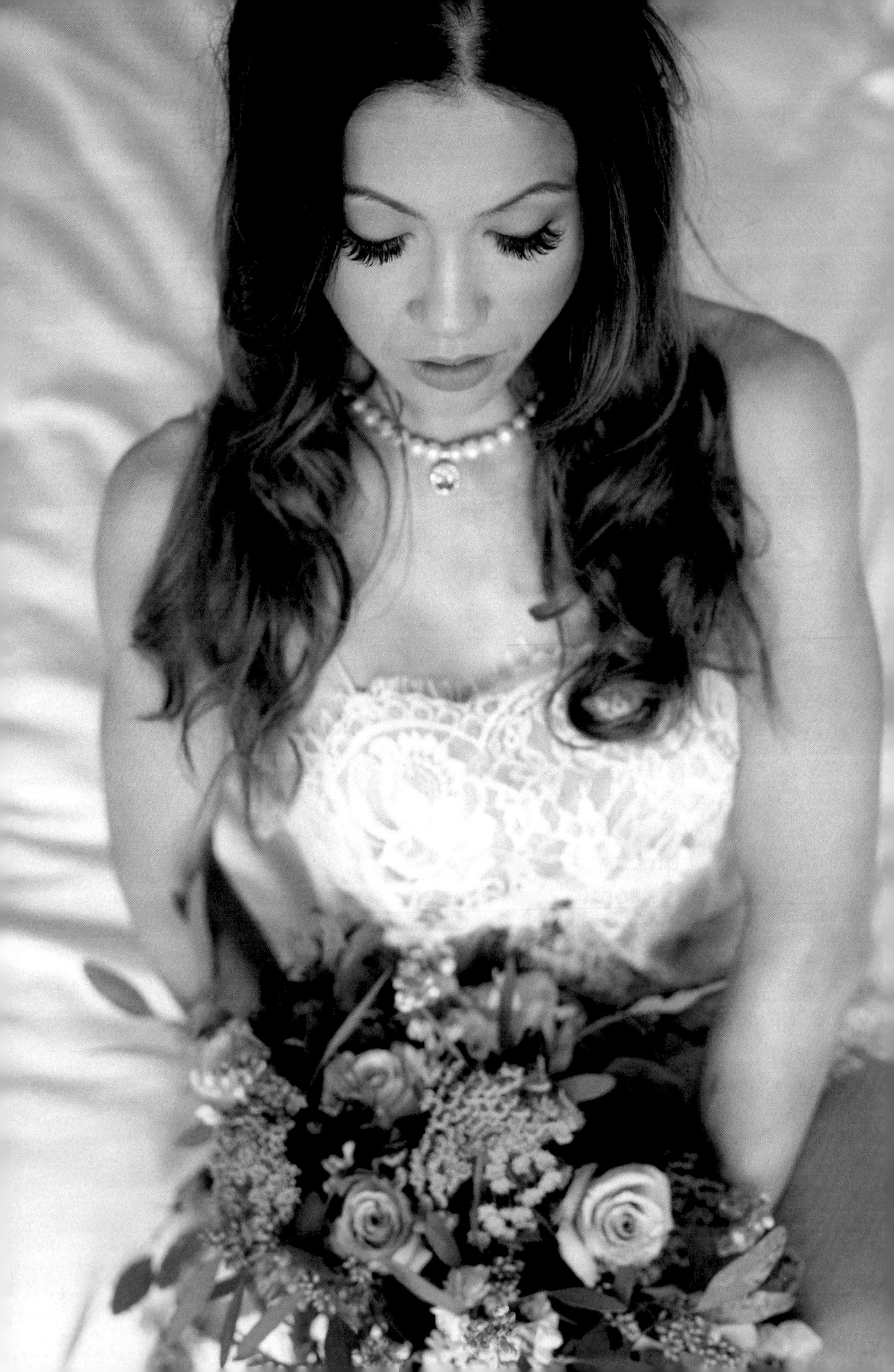

'Our dark days allow us to feel the sunshine.
Diversity is divine; our flaws make us appreciate our beauty.
Stop trying to please others, just please yourself.
We are perfectly imperfect.
Stand up, be heard, roar in your own way, but most of all, be who you
are, not who you think the world wants you to be.
You are not broken, you are mending. You are worthy, wonderful and
beautiful in every single way.'
~ Sophie Mei Lan

Society and those around you may depict your role or purpose; for example, mother, wife, business owner, journalist...

Finding my 'why' has been critical to my self-development. I had to remove the shackles of being identified solely as a 'journalist' or a 'mum', because no single label fully defines me.

Discovering that I could make a positive change in the world, by talking openly about my history and mental health problems, gives me a sense of purpose. Blogging and vlogging allows me to use my journalistic skills, as well as giving me the flexibility to be Mum to my beautiful girls.

Running my own media channels gives me control over my future. At first, my blog was purely a way to express myself and record my thoughts surrounding my mental health and motherhood. I quickly realised that, whilst my personal experience can be comforting to, and useful for, others in similar situations, I needed to talk directly to those people. I needed to help them as well as myself.

Typically, my vlog covers such topics as attachment parenting, mental health and everything in-between, but I wanted to add even more value. I actively collaborated with others and made the decision to show the raw parts of my life when they cropped up — the not so pretty parts, like when I had a panic attack and/ or suicidal thoughts, evidence of my self-esteem issues, and some of the thinking behind my eating disorder.

Whilst it is truly a dream job — one that didn't even exist when I was growing up — I still find it difficult. I'm driven forward because I can see the greatness in being a force for good as well as how inspirational it can be for others when they see you being true to yourself.

*

When I was on benefits, receiving state handouts and food vouchers, in-between working for the national news, I was encouraged to get a 'proper job'.

When I went to the Job Centre, I was encouraged to go on business courses that were led by tutors who had never run a business.

When I won business awards and contracts, I was commended for going against the norm.

When I was belly-dancing, I was told to practise 'proper dancing', rather than the 'prostitution' I was apparently peddling.

When I was on telly and dubbed 'Britain's best belly-dancer', and told by Simon Cowell that I had 'absolute star quality', I was championed by curvy women. People loved my rags to riches story.

When I became a mum, I was given lots of handbooks and advice on discipline and 'crying it out' techniques. I was told that I was 'creating a rod for my own back' by being a gentle parent. After training as a breastfeeding peer supporter and blogging about attachment parenting, I was paraded by health bodies and brands as a 'gentle parenting ambassador'.

When I started out in journalism, I was told to make friends with people in power. When I won 'scoop of the year' and human rights journalism awards, I was praised for giving a voice to the seldom heard.

The times when I've been judged and pushed to follow the crowd proved to be defining moments in my life; despite initially struggling I ultimately blossomed.

On all those occasions, the only constant was me. I eventually discovered the positives from each situation and trusted my instincts, drive and passion — even if it meant going against the grain.

I truly believe that, without darkness, there is no light. If I could leave you with any advice, it would be: have the courage to follow your own path in life.

*

Over time, my blog and vlog grew. They began to take over my journalism work.

I've found my voice and community online, collaborating with brands that I love and becoming a spokesperson in the media for motherhood and mental health issues.

I've won awards for my mental health campaigns. I share my story, as a public speaker, and I've become a role model for recovery. I still teach dance in communities and performed at gigs as a belly-dancer and Samba dancer.

Whilst rediscovering success in a new, more wholesome way has been great, I've had to be careful not to slip back into my workaholic ways. I've had to be careful that the online world doesn't take over my real life and start to negatively impact my mental health.

That said, social media is 24/7 and I've often been breastfeeding whilst simultaneously posting on my channels. I constantly update my social media content then stay up late finishing off blogs and vlogs.

I do love it. It's genuinely flexible for family life, though I have to be strict with myself to be 'present' and attentive when I'm with my girls, as it can be addictive. I feel my current career uses my journalistic and presenting skills whilst also fulfilling my passion to help others.

Whilst it may sound as if my life is now sorted, that's not how mental health works. It's an ongoing process, and though I do feel I'm in a much better place than I was, the bully can still raise her head when she wants to.

Thankfully, I now have so many mechanisms to drown out her voice — positive habits, hobbies, thought processes and more. I only have to remember that true wealth is health…not the trolling and constant judgement of others, or the current negative addiction I'm likely to be worrying about.

I can't stop life throwing a spanner in the works or putting obstacles in my way — that's unrealistic. I don't expect to be fully 'healed' for the rest of my days without experiencing any hiccups or relapses.

All I know is that I am worthy of the love of my daughters, and my family and friends.

*And, just as importantly, I love **me**. I am worthy of my **own** admiration, dedication and loyalty.*

Epilogue

Sat at my laptop, the bright screen illuminating my face, I try to concentrate on what I'm writing. Inside, I'm panicking because I'm snacking. My keyboard is sticky from the food residue on my fingers.

I know I shouldn't be eating at my computer. I've heard this countless times…how you need to be mindful when eating. But I also know that those snacks are keeping me going and helping me to write. I don't feel I deserve to eat unless I'm doing something.

Just one more paragraph, one more snack. I feel so guilty. I've only been to the gym once today, and now I'm undoing all my hard work by snacking. But I'm against a deadline and I need to finish this work.

The wave is rising inside me. I tell others to ride the wave. I know it's my anxiety from overeating. It feels too much. I'm drowning.

I keep eating and working and downing fizzy drinks. When I'm about to explode I'll make myself sick. I'll tell myself it's just a one-off. I'm so torn…I can't break months of no purging, but I also can't live with snacking so much.

That's it, I'm done. I've finished this paragraph. Now I can rush to the toilet.

Tap on, head over the toilet bowl, fingers down throat. It's been a while, but the process is ingrained. In a few moments I'll be free. Let's just hope I can bring everything back up so that I can return to my laptop without feeling full.

Finally, it's all out. I know most of the calories remain inside me, but at least vomiting has tempered my anxiety and I'm free again. Back to work now.

*

Like many people, I've always dreamt of writing a book. I've forever been determined that each trial and tribulation I experienced would be part of my autobiography. Here I am, writing that very book…but it's not been as easy as I thought.

I'm always on the go and I struggle to stay still. This is partly the bully inside me exerting her control—making me feel that I'm undeserving of a sit down or fearing a short rest in case I gain weight. Also, whenever I do sit down, I realise how hungry I am, so I eat.

During the years spent writing this book I've snacked <u>a lot</u>. I've tried to write in short bursts, like high intensity interval training—but, often, when you get stuck into something, it's hard to do that; as a result, I've snacked and snacked.

This has messed with my brain. I normally only eat when I'm hungry, and I'm careful about stopping when I'm full.

I won't lie and say that writing this book has been purely therapeutic. It has in the sense that I've realised how far I've come—and I hope that, even if you feel you're a few steps behind me, you know there's an amazing future ahead.

Recovery is not an upward trajectory, even in the latter stages, which is where I am today. With any addiction, whether it's working, alcohol, food, social media, gambling, etc., you may feel that you've recovered, then one day you find out how easy it is to relapse.

If I down a shot of alcohol, something I rarely touch, I'll throw it back and feel free again. So, I'll have another shot. And another. And another. That familiar, carefree, woozy head takes over and it feels like a good idea. Just like old times, when I regularly put metaphorical sticking plasters over my deepest wounds.

Deep down, I know this isn't the way to go, but I do it anyway. I'm hurting. I'm in pain. I persuade myself that I need this relief. It's been a tough time, after all. I'm owed this release.

Before I know it, I begin to re-enact my former life. I put on my party girl mask.

The next day, the mask is off. I feel a crippling anxiety like no other. I berate myself. I analyse every moment and interaction I can remember. I feel guilty…am I always going to revert to dark times? Will I ever recover?

That was me the other night, though I'm sure many people will identify with the process. But we **must not** beat ourselves up. It happens. I feel sad that I went back there, but I'm also grateful that I can see why it happened and where things went wrong. This is my story. Your story. Our journey.

I must be proud of myself that my cycles of self-destruction are much shorter and less intense than they used to be. I may have a blip, even though I know I can prevent one.

We're only human. The worst thing we can do is feel shame. We may feel guilty about our actions, but, please, try not to feel shame.

We should treat ourselves like we'd treat a friend who's struggling. I would never berate a friend if they lapsed; I'd check how they were and understand that they must have been having a really tough time.

I will continue to build my resilience to such blips — because that's all they are now, blips, not weeks of self-loathing and endless cycles of addictive behaviour. I realise that recovery means a glitch every now and again, but that these brief regressions can be a positive reminder of how far I've come and where I absolutely do not want to return to.

We must learn to ride the waves, but we also need to be patient. We can only do our best, and we must identify our individual triggers and learn how to avoid them or — better still — diminish them.

Writing this book was a constant trigger. Rather than find continual solace in food, I'd distract myself by cleaning, tidying or doing something else for ten minutes until the wave passed.

Life is all about gaining knowledge and experience. However, it's through our mistakes that we learn our best lessons.

Recovery from addiction can only come from within. We need to learn to accept ourselves, but also love ourselves a little bit more each day. We may need help to do this, until we can ultimately take control. Not false control through temporary 'crutches' — real control of our lives on this planet. Remember: we can only control our own actions, not those of others.

You've shown you have the strength to do this — through your work, through your addiction(s), through your battles in life. Now it's your time. Don't let the bully inside control how you think, feel or act. It's time to find the loving friend within you.

That friend who will be there when you make mistakes.

The friend who will always be your cheerleader.

The friend who will remind you that failures lead to success.

The friend that will alter your language from 'can't' to <u>can</u>.

The friend you deserve.

Be your own unconditional friend.

Live a life of sparkles and smiles. Forgive and be set free.

Peace, love and shimmies!
Sophie Mei Lan

About the Author

Sophie Mei Lan is a multi-award-winning vlogger, blogger and qualified journalist who specialises in mental health and wellbeing; she has worked for local and national press and achieved international acclaim for her work.

Since setting up her own family, mental health and lifestyle blog in 2015, Mama Mei (MamaMei.co.uk), she has regularly appeared on television and in the press, including: ITV's Good Morning Britain, BBC Two's Victoria Derbyshire Show, The Independent, Metro and Grazia Magazine. She is also a regular contributor on BBC radio.

As well as founding the Evoke Media Group with her friend and business partner Daria Ni., Sophie launched the Blog Up North (the Ultimate Guide to the North of England) magazine and influencer network as well as Yorkshire Families magazine.

She began vlogging professionally in 2017. Her YouTube channel has 43k subscribers and more than 19 million views (youtube.com/SophieMeiLan).

In addition to creating videos for clients and the media via Evoke, Sophie is a broadcast journalist for BBC News and Channel 4 News. She also writes regular columns for various newspapers and online publications.

Awards:

- Amnesty International Human Rights Media Award
- IRN Commercial Radio Award
- Blog Of the Year 2020
- PR Week Campaign for Good Award 2019
- Influencer of the Year 2018
- Various NCTJ Awards